MODERN ROUTING TECHNIQUES

First published in Great Britain by the Trade Division
of Unwin Hyman Limited, 1990

UNWIN HYMAN LIMITED
15–17 Broadwick Street
London W1V 1FP

Allen & Unwin Australia Pty Ltd
8 Napier Street, North Sydney, NSW 2060, Australia

**Allen & Unwin New Zealand Pty Ltd with the Port
Nicholson Press**
Compusales Building, 75 Ghuznee Street,
Wellington, New Zealand

British Library Cataloguing in Publication Data
Philips, Jim
  Advanced routing techniques.
  1. Power woodworking tools
  I. Title II. Perkins, John
  621.9'3

  ISBN 0–04–440196–5

Designed by Colin Lewis & Associates

Printed and bound in Great Britain by
Butler & Tanner Ltd, Frome and London

MODERN ROUTING
TECHNIQUES

MODERN ROUTING TECHNIQUES

JIM PHILLIPS
AND JOHN PERKINS

UNWIN
HYMAN

LONDON SYDNEY WELLINGTON

First published in Great Britain by the Trade Division
of Unwin Hyman Limited, 1990

UNWIN HYMAN LIMITED
15–17 Broadwick Street
London W1V 1FP

Allen & Unwin Australia Pty Ltd
8 Napier Street, North Sydney, NSW 2060, Australia

**Allen & Unwin New Zealand Pty Ltd with the Port
Nicholson Press**
Compusales Building, 75 Ghuznee Street,
Wellington, New Zealand

British Library Cataloguing in Publication Data
Philips, Jim
   Advanced routing techniques.
   1. Power woodworking tools
   I. Title   II. Perkins, John
   621.9'3

   ISBN 0–04–440196–5

Designed by Colin Lewis & Associates

Printed and bound in Great Britain by
Butler & Tanner Ltd, Frome and London

Contents

Acknowledgements

The authors would like to acknowledge the assistance provided by a number of people.

On the technical side, John Tigg and his assistant, Neil McMillan, gave a valued contribution. On the artistic side, Annette Kelly and her colleague, Emma Hughes, worked like beavers to get the cutters illustrated on schedule.

The authors' thanks go to David Scammell for his excellent technical illustrations. The advice and encouragement from John Costello and John Bonnet was also immensely helpful.

An Introduction to the Portable Electric Router

Few modern tools have had such an impact on woodworking practice as the portable electric router. Furthermore, it is an impact not restricted to any particular level, but equally shared across the whole range of associated woodworking crafts: from the building construction and mass-produced furniture industries, to specialist trades such as shopfitting, restoration and boatbuilding, through to the work of the home craftsman and DIY enthusiast. The secret behind this success is the router's versatility, simplicity and convenience.

However, this mild revolution has not happened overnight, for it has taken some 40 years, during which time the router has slowly and gradually developed into the highly efficient machine available today.

Much of this development obviously relates to advancements in the design of compact high-speed, high-power electric motors and, more recently, the use of electronic speed control and stabilization. These, combined with many other design innovations, have succeeded in making the portable electric router both safer and easier to handle and therefore far more acceptable to both the amateur and professional craftsman.

Following this wider acceptance, the ancillary technology behind routing has also developed and grown to provide for specialist requirements such as the composition of high performance cutter materials, precision jigs and guide systems and the development of specialized routing machines to suit the needs of many different industries handling many different materials.

The electric router offers the facility to cut and shape timber and other materials to a high standard and quality of finish. The type of work that can now be achieved with the modern router is extremely varied, ranging from simple rebating and grooving, to complex shaping, trimming and jointing operations which in the past have required less versatile and often far more expensive equipment, or time-consuming hand techniques.

Router Power

(see also power/speed table, page 23)

Portable electric routers can be categorized into four basic groups according to their power rating and therefore, to some extent, the type of work that they are most suited to. However, most professional quality routers are capable of being used for a wide and varying range of machining operations, power limitations mainly being relevant to the frequency of use, the size of cutter to be used, and the speed with which the whole operation can be carried out. When considering or comparing the power rating of particular makes and models, it is necessary to bear in mind that it is the output rating that is important. The difference between power input and output and the machine's ultimate efficiency is greatly dependent upon the standard of design and manufacture of the machine itself.

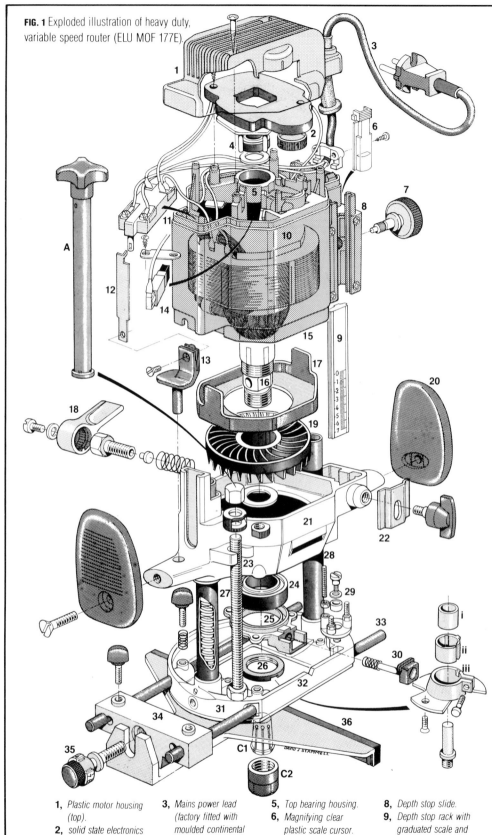

FIG. 1 Exploded illustration of heavy duty, variable speed router (ELU MOF 177E).

10, *Armature windings and commutator assembly.*
11, *On/off switch.*
A, *Fine depth adjuster (optional equipment).*
12, *Switch operating link.*
13, *Switch slide button.*
14, *Motor brushes (either side of commutator).*
15, *Plastic motor housing.*
16, *Shaft threaded and drilled to take collet and collet nut and drilled for shaft lock.*
17, *Ventilation ducting shield.*
18, *Plunge column clamping lever (operating against plunge column).*
19, *Cooling fan.*
20, *Side handles.*
21, *Combined metal lower motor casing, bottom shaft bearing housing, plunge carriage and side handle arms.*
22, *Adjustable depth stop clamp.*
23, *Stroke return stop with quick release nut.*
i, *Retractable template guide bush.*
ii, *Guide bush sleeve.*
iii, *Guide bush clamping collar and mounting plate.*
24, *Lower shaft bearing.*
25, *Lower bearing plate and shaft lock housing.*
26, *Threaded bearing cap.*
27, *Plunge column with internal carriage return spring.*
28, *Plunge column with internal carriage return spring.*
29, *Rotating turret stop.*
30, *Shaft lock engaging pin and button.*
31, *Router base.*
32, *Plastic facing plate.*
33, *Side fence rods.*
34, *Side fence clamping bar.*
35, *Fine adjuster for side fence.*
36, *Side fence with adjustable face linings.*
C1, *Collet (various size collects available to suit standard cutter shank diameters.*
C2, *Collet locknut.*

1, *Plastic motor housing (top).*
2, *solid state electronics and variable speed control dial.*
3, *Mains power lead (factory fitted with moulded continental plug).*
4, *Top shaft bearing.*
5, *Top bearing housing.*
6, *Magnifying clear plastic scale cursor.*
7, *Adjustable depth stop pinion/control knob.*
8, *Depth stop slide.*
9, *Depth stop rack with graduated scale and threaded adjustable foot.*

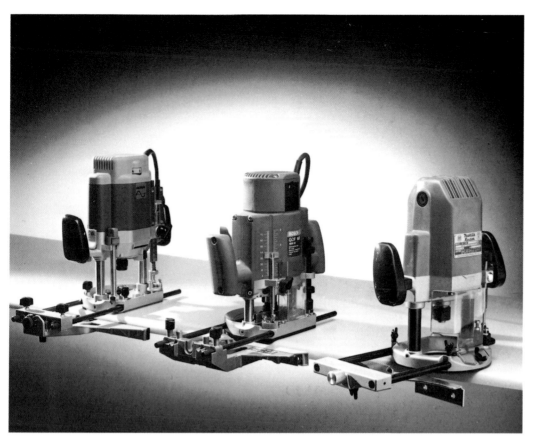

LEFT Fig. 2a Many power tool manufacturers now offer a range of routers varying in power, capacity and price including industrial models such as those shown from ELU (Black & Decker), Bosch, and Makita.

▲ **FIG. 2a** · ▼ **FIG. 2b**

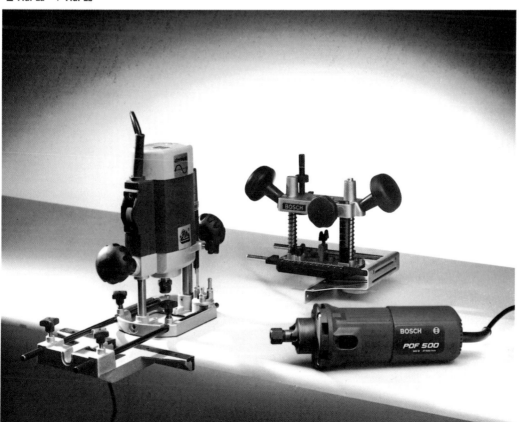

LEFT Fig. 2b Lower powered routers are not intended (other than those designated as DIY) as a cheaper alternative to the larger models, but offer lighter and easier control for many free hand and intricate detailing operations.

Plunge Action

The introduction of the plunge router, with its many operational and safety advantages, has to some extent precluded the use and availability of depth-fed routers in the UK and throughout the EEC. However, depth-fed routers are still widely used in the USA and other areas, both as handheld machines and in conjunction with specific proprietary jigs, or as specialized single-purpose machines. As routing technology progresses we may well see the re-introduction of depth-fed routers for the latter purpose on a wider scale. Particular examples are laminate trimming and mitring machines (see page 104) which require the facility to be pre-set to a precise cutting depth, as well as door lock mortising machines (see page 94), and panel routers (see page 49).

The advantage of the plunge action is in its precision and stability when feeding the cutter into the work and for most routing operations in its withdrawal of the cutter above the baseplate when released. The latter safety aspect has led to a much greater acceptance of the router by health and safety officers for use in industrial and other commercial workshops. The precision of the plunge stroke and stability of the wide base also ensures that the cutter enters and retracts from the cut at 90° to the surface, producing a clean square cut, not oval or chipped out around the edge.

In use, the open carriage of the plunge action router allows good vision when positioning the base on the work, aligning the cutter at the start of the cut and of any directional or stop markings on the face.

Heavy Duty

With input power ratings from 1,500 watts (approximately 2HP), heavy duty routers offer far greater efficiency, being able to cut deeper and wider in a single pass, having a greater plunge cutting depth, and generally, as expected, being far more robust and less likely to be overloaded through misuse. However, they are larger and bulkier machines to handle and are fairly costly, both in themselves and in the types and size of cutters most suited for use with them or required to realize their full potential. They are generally necessary for applications such

Light Duty

For home craftsmen and craft workshops as well as for many industrial uses, light duty routers around 600 watts or more (approximately 0·8HP) are most suited for use with the comprehensive range of 6·5mm shank cutters, offering the ease of handling and versatility required to carry out a wide range of general purpose and decorative routing operations. They are particularly ideal for applications involving intricate work such as applying decorative mouldings, inlay grooves and rebates, and free-hand machining and carving.

DIY

DIY routers are generally designed at a price to suit a particular market and the quality of individual models designated as DIY varies considerably. Beware of the cheaper machines, often producing inadequate power under load and lacking stability in the construction of the base and fence arrangement, the latter allowing play or movement that can cause inaccuracy in the finished work. However, better quality DIY routers offer good value and are ideally suited for infrequent use, where a light-weight, easily handled machine is required. However, limitations in cutting capacity can be disappointing.

as the production of building joinery (stair-cases, windows, doorframes etc.) and other fairly heavy or continuous operations. For these applications 12·7mm diameter shank cutters are to be preferred, although alternative size collets are either supplied or available for most makes of machine.

Medium Duty
Routers of over 1000 watts (approximately 1·3HP) offer a good compromise between power and durability and are ideal in workshop situations where 6·35, 9·5, and 12·7mm shank cutters are in general use. Being slightly more compact and convenient to handle than the heavier duty models, they are often used for both general routing operations in the workshop and for cutting and trimming operations, such as those involving laminate-faced worktops in the installation of fitted kitchens and other similar on-site work.

Plunge Lock and Depth Gauge
One of two methods of locking the plunge carriage at the required cutting depth is generally adopted, using either one of the side handles as a clamping screw, or by means of a separate clamping lever that can be released by thumb and/or finger pressure without letting go of the side handle. In either case, the action must be as light and positive as possible, with minimal movement to prevent any delay in locking or releasing.

Most plunge routers are fitted with an adjustable depth stop to allow precise setting of the plunge stroke. This consists of a locking slide rod or bar that sits against a stop on the router base. On professional, quality routers a graduated scale is often incorporated to allow the cutting depth to be easily read off and reset, while on more expensive models the bar is adjusted by means of a rack and pinion operated by a control knob on the side of the machine. For some routing operations, however, it is necessary to eliminate the plunge action and set and lock the cutter at a precise depth of cut. To achieve this, a fine depth setting screw can be fitted between the sliding carriage and base of the router (see Fig. 1).

On depth fed routers, the router base consists of a cylindrical casting into which the motor and collet assembly slides. The depth of cut is then set by raising or lowering the motor assembly in the base, by means of rack and pinion gearing, threaded body ring or other screw adjustment. With depth fed routers, the depth of cut is set and locked prior to the cutter being fed into the work, making it far more difficult to plunge centred and square into the work. When feeding into the edge of the work, this system creates no problem but does leave the cutter dangerously exposed as it leaves the cut, up until it slows and stops. Resetting the depth of cut is generally slower than with plunge routers, in particular, those having multi-position turret stops.

Turret Stop
Many plunge routers are now fitted with three position turret stops on which the depth gauge rod sits. This consists of a rotating turret, carrying three adjustable screw stops of varying heights, which can be set to limit the depth of cut on each subsequent pass, the total being equal to the required depth of cut.

Speed Control
Many routers are now available with variable electronic speed control, allowing the operator to vary the speed to suit the characteristics of the material being worked, the cutter type and diameter, and the operation being performed.

Although variable electronic speed control on power tools is now fairly common, there are several different methods of achieving it. However, with routers, maintaining a constant spindle speed under load is of utmost importance in preventing burn marks and producing a good finish. To achieve this a closed loop electronic system is generally used which incorporates a feed back system to monitor the armature speed and automatically increases or decreases the input power to maintain a constant speed pre-set by the operator.

The most accurate feed back system in general use is Tachometric feedback whereby a radially magnetized transmitter is mounted on the armature shaft and a pick-up mounted close to it. As the transmitter rotates the pick-up generates a voltage of variable frequency which is measured and used as a speed variation signal by the control circuit to monitor the actual speed and regulate it to keep it constant.

A particular characteristic of this system is the slow speed pick-up when the machine is switched on, generally referred to as 'soft start'. This is due to this monitoring effect, the electronic circuit smoothly controlling the power increase up to the required preset speed. Slow start routers are often criticized by operators more used to single speed machines which reach working speed without this delay. However, it does eliminate the harsh starting kick of single speed machines and they tend to run smoother and therefore more quietly.

To produce a clean precise cut while maintaining its compact lightweight manageability, the handheld electric router relies on high speed rather than the power as available from a heavy stationary machine motor such as fitted to a spindle moulder. With lower power router motors the no-load running speed is generally around 24,000 to 28,000 RPM, with heavy duty models at around 20,000 to 22,000 RPM. Variable speed routers generally range from 8,000 to 24,000 and 8,000 to 20,000 RPM respectively. Speed control dials are often graduated in single numbers rather than actual speed settings (a better system featured on Porter Cable (USA) routers uses a digital readout to indicate the true speed range), but these do not always relate to the same speed range on all routers due to the variations in power rating and the different relationship between the power and speed curve of specific motors. It is therefore necessary to check (manufacturer's handbook) the precise setting for each specific speed band (8,000, 10,000 RPM etc.).

Ease of Handling

As with all power and hand tools, it is essential for a router to be comfortable to hold and easy to handle. It must be well balanced, its base being large enough to prevent it tipping when being fed into the work and giving enough support to keep the machine upright when overhanging work during edge trimming or machining operations. Bases having one flat side are to be preferred, as these allow the cutter to be run closer to a straight edge or guide while still providing adequate support when edge cutting.

The ergonomics of the design of the side handles does tend to vary from router to router, ranging from smooth round knobs to long tear-shaped handles. In practice, most operators can quickly get used to handling the different types, although preference often depends on hand size and the personally adopted attitude of holding a router. In preference, I would suggest somewhere between the two: handles which offer a smooth comfortable grip from either side, as well as from above the machine, but which are squared or elongated enough to prevent the machine from turning in the hands. One of the advantages of the depth fed router is that the side handles are fitted to the base of the router, and therefore, much lower down than on plunge action routers, giving better balance and control. When free-hand carving or producing similar detailed work, it is often better to disregard the plunge action and control the router from a lower point. Depth-fed, heavy duty, industrial routers are often fitted with one or both side handles of the pistol grip type, providing a firmer grip on these extremely powerful, and correspondingly, less easy to handle machines.

On-off switches should be smooth in operation but with positive positions, and easily operated by the thumb or finger without the need to let go of the side handle. There is at present some call to introduce dead-man style release switches on routers as a safety measure. This has been met with some scepticism from many experienced router users, concerned at the possible problems in maintaining a constant uninterrupted cutter speed during more complex or awkward routing operations. Speed control dials should be positioned in such a way that they cannot be moved accidentally during the cutting operation.

Collets
The most common method used to align and retain the parallel cutter shank in the motor

shaft is to hold it in a split collet, itself having a matching taper fit into the end of the shaft (see Fig. 3). A lock nut is then used to both tighten the taper and close the split collet to grip the cutter shank. To prevent vibration, which will result in uneven and inaccurate cutting as well as possible damage to the machine itself, the collet must be initially machined and maintained to ensure perfect alignment along the central axis of the shaft and cutter. This is often a major fault on cheaper and less sophisticated machines.

To accommodate different cutter shank diameters, equivalent diameter inter-changeable collets are available to fit most professional routers.

An alternative method of retaining the cutter is used on some CNC and other industrial machines whereby the shaft is threaded to take an internally threaded cutter shank. This allows faster and easier cutter changing on multiple head machines or during long runs of repetitive batch work.

Health and Safety

Rather than present the reader with a formidable list of safety Dos and Don'ts, and in the hope that they are more likely to be noticed and taken note of, we have inserted safe working reminders in the form of safety tips at relative points throughout the book. However, it is not only the practicalities of handling tools such as the electric router that present danger to both new and experienced craftsmen but often the not so obvious health hazards such as the effects of inhaling fine airborne waste particles or the effects of excessive continuous noise.

Dust Extraction

Increased publicity has led to a far greater awareness of and concern about the dangers of inhaling dust and waste particles during machining and surface-finishing operations. This in turn has led manufacturers to develop and market extraction equipment for use with their tools (and often other manufacturers') designed to reduce and minimize the health risk, thereby encouraging the wider and more acceptable use of specialized machinery, and power tools at all levels of craft and construction work.

▲ **FIG. 4**

ABOVE Fig. 4 Vacuum extraction of dust and chips not only greatly reduces the health risk but helps prevent waste and swarf packing around the cutter and raising the cutting edge temperature.

One manufacturer which has shown particular concern over this problem is ELU (part of the professional tool division of Black & Decker), who now offer a complete and efficient extraction system to supplement their extensive router and router accessory range (see Fig. 4). It is also worth noting that the ELU range of dust-extraction and general routing equipment is further extended by many specialized items offered by Trend, developed in close consultation with ELU themselves.

In operation electric routers generally produce extremely fine waste particles, in contrast to the coarse chips generated by planing and spindle-moulding equipment. This necessitates the use of high-velocity low-volume (HVLV) extraction equipment, the high-velocity vacuum removing the waste more effectively from the immediate

▲ FIG. 5

ABOVE Fig. 5 Fitted to inverted machines dust extraction also reduces the risk of fine waste falling into the ventilation slots in the router body, a common cause of router failure.

cutting area (low-velocity high-volume (HVLV) extraction units are better suited to removing dust or larger waste particles emitted over a wider area and are of little benefit when using high-speed routers). When using a vacuum extractor for dust removal the same unit should not be connected via a Y-junction to a vacuum chuck.

The open cutting action of a router tends to throw out waste material in all directions. It is therefore necessary to extract it from as close to the cutter as possible – preferably, for maximum efficiency, by enclosing it within a transparent hood. Generally this hood, with the hose connector, is a separate fitting, held in place by one of the side fence rods. Unfortunately, this can sometimes obscure the operator's view of the cutter and get in the way when changing cutters. It is to be hoped that with time dust extraction

facilities will be designed as an integral part of the router, making it simpler and less of an obstruction to use for all operations. On routers of the later ELU 177 and 96 ranges the problem of cutter changing has been simplified by the integral shaft lock, while regular use of compressed air and a drop of antistatic fluid (as used on gramophone records) will tend to keep the hood reasonably clear.

Extract ports can also be built into or attached to guide fences, jigs and router bases (see Fig. 5), though these are rarely as efficient as fitted hood extractors.

Dust Masks, Eye Protection and Ear Defenders

There is often a greater tendency for the router operator to lean over the machine or peer closely at the cutter to see what it is doing than with other types of machine cutting equipment. It is therefore essential when using an electric router to take as many safety precautions as possible. Also, certain natural materials, even some species of timber, as well as most metals and metal compounds, and many man-made materials, preservative treatments, and surface coatings can have harmful effects, as a result of toxic, immunological and carcinogenic properties.

If dust-extraction facilities are not available (or, with dangerous or very dusty materials, even if they are) do wear a dust mask. The shaped throwaway and the aluminium-framed refill type (I find the former more comfortable) are both suitable, although more specific toxic respirators should be worn if the material is particularly irritant or asphyxiant. Do check with material manufacturers and health authorities if there is any doubt about the safety of working with a particular material.

Not only is there likely to be waste material from the workpiece flying about but it is not unknown for a tip or part of the cutter to come adrift or for the cutter to come loose. Safety glasses or a visor should be worn during all cutting operations. Visors are best as they also protect the face and allow all-round vision. To avoid scratching clear plastic visors or lenses, blow the dust off them with compressed air before wiping over lightly with an antistatic lens cloth.

The noise emitted by a high-speed router over a continuous period can not only be harmful to the ears, but also highly irritating, resulting in a loss of concentration in the operator and other workers in the same area, which leads to accidents and mistakes, and so affects the quality of the finished work. Ear muffs or defenders should therefore be worn by the operator and also by other people close to the routing operation. When using variable-speed routers never set the speed low to reduce the noise level. Always cut at the most efficient cutter speed to suit the material and operation.

Safety Tip

Always work in a well lit area with an even spread of light over the work surface to avoid deceptive shadows or glare.

Safety Tip

Regularly check the condition of the power lead and replace it if it is badly worn or kinked. Always ensure that cable of the correct power rating is used for tools and extension leads.

1 Techniques of Working with the Handheld Router

The main advantages of the electric router over conventional hand-cutting methods are the speed and precision with which it enables many previously time-consuming operations such as dovetailing, tenoning or even simple edge trimming to be carried out. But in order to use the router to its full advantage and continue to achieve consistently good results it is necessary to plan exactly how you are going to proceed through any operation assessing all problems that are likely to occur. These may include the sequence in which you carry out each stage to minimize cutter or machine resetting, which edges to cut first to avoid or reduce grain breakout, or what extra support is needed to ensure that the router continues smoothly and level as it runs into and out of the cut. Obviously, before you switch on to start cutting, there are, as with all power tools or machines, various safety checks to make as covered by the safety reminders shown in boxes throughout this book.

Each operation involved in producing a particular item or set of matching components will differ, but the basic considerations in handling and setting up the router and workpiece will be similar.

As with all machine tools, the process of setting up the router, jig making and/or securing the workpiece is generally far more time-consuming than actually making the cut. Therefore, when constructing a piece of furniture or any item consisting of several or multiple components, it is worth while planning out all operations, grouping together those that can be carried out in one operation or similar operations so as to involve the minimum machine setting-up and resetting time. Similarly, when time and the economics of the job allow, aim to design jigs and templates to be as versatile as possible in allowing several components to be cut at a time, to take materials of various sizes and for possible reuse on similar future projects.

Setting Up and Cutting with the Handheld Router

Much of the setting-up time of spindle moulders and other shaping machines is spent in fitting and aligning the cutter knives. With the router this is virtually done in the grinding of the cutter itself, requiring only the selection and fitting of the cutter of the required profile in the collet.

When selecting cutters always use the largest diameter possible or one of the same diameter as the width of cut. Avoid cutters under 6mm diameter whenever possible as these are far more likely to snap under normal routing conditions. Similarly, always opt for 9·5mm or 12·7mm shank sizes, in particular when the cutter diameter is larger than the shank diameter. Always fit the cutter into the collet by the full recommended length and never attempt to work with a blunt or damaged cutter (see Cutter Problems, page 125).

To avoid vibration the collet must be set

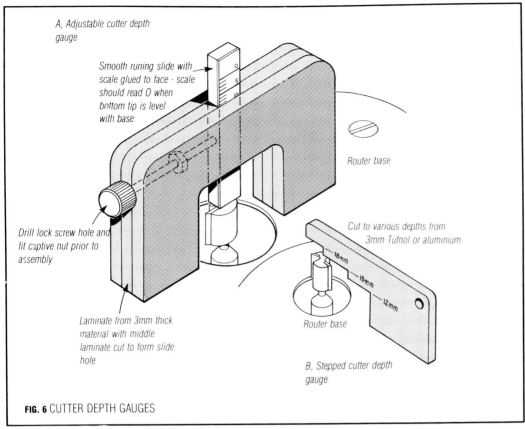

A, Adjustable cutter depth gauge

Smooth runing slide with scale glued to face · scale should read 0 when bottom tip is level with base

Router base

Drill lock screw hole and fit captive nut prior to assembly

Cut to various depths from 3mm Tufnol or aluminium

Laminate from 3mm thick material with middle laminate cut to form slide hole

Router base

B, Stepped cutter depth gauge

FIG. 6 CUTTER DEPTH GAUGES

▲ FIG. 6

centrally and in line with the shaft. Regularly check the condition (see Collet Maintenance, page 121) of the collet and clean the shaft seating, cap threads and collet side slots. Before inserting the cutter check that there are no burrs, pitting or ovality in the shank and that the collet cap thread does not bind.

Hold the shaft with the open-ended spanner provided (do ensure that it is a close fit across the shaft flats to avoid rounding the corners) or with the spindle lock fitted to the later ELU MOF 177(E) and 96(E) models (see Fig. 1). On some low-power routers, the shaft is locked by a steel pin inserted through the shaft locating in a groove on the router body. Always ensure that the pin is removed before switching on as the torque imposed could damage the motor or shaft or throw the pin out at high speed. With the cap spanner (again check the fit) slacken off the collet cap. On all ELU routers the collets have a double safety lock, the collet appearing to tighten then releasing before finally tightening. Do ensure that you reach both stages.

Setting the Depth of Cut

On most plunge routers the depth of cut is set by a rod or slide, seating against either a fixed or a three-position turret stop on the base and locked at the required depth by a thumbscrew. For fine setting a few of the larger routers such as the ELU MOF 177 have a toothed slide operated through a geared knob. On many machines the depth of cut can be read off a graduated scale against a cursor on the slide or column. However, it is generally better to set the depth using the fitting or material itself or with a cutter gauge (see Fig. 6), relying on the machine scale only for approximate step settings.

With low-power routers (up to 750 watts input) the full depth of cut should be achieved in steps of about 3–4mm when using cutters below 6·3mm in diameter, increasing to 6mm steps for cutters over 6·3mm. As an approximate guide, the depth of each step should not exceed the cutter diameter. However, only experience can tell the limits to which it is safe to load the router, taking into account the characteris-

Safety Tip

Do not overtighten the collet as it damages the cutter shank (see collet and router maintenance page 120).

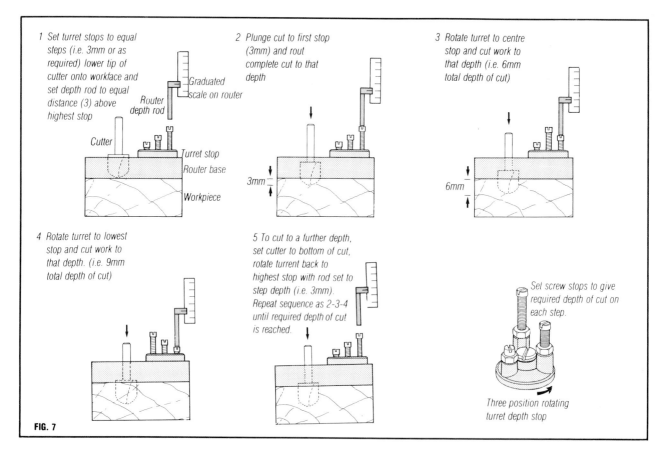

1 Set turret stops to equal steps (i.e. 3mm or as required) lower tip of cutter onto workface and set depth rod to equal distance (3) above highest stop

Graduated scale on router

Router depth rod

Cutter

Turret stop

Router base

Workpiece

2 Plunge cut to first stop (3mm) and rout complete cut to that depth

3mm

3 Rotate turret to centre stop and cut work to that depth (i.e. 6mm total depth of cut)

6mm

4 Rotate turret to lowest stop and cut work to that depth. (i.e. 9mm total depth of cut)

5 To cut to a further depth, set cutter to bottom of cut, rotate turrent back to highest stop with rod set to step depth (i.e. 3mm). Repeat sequence as 2-3-4 until required depth of cut is reached.

Set screw stops to give required depth of cut on each step.

Three position rotating turret depth stop

FIG. 7

tics of the materials being handled. With more powerful routers a limit of 3mm should be maintained for cutters or cutters with 6.35mm shanks. As a general guide when using heavy duty routers with cutters having shank diameters of 9·5mm or 12·7mm, the depth of cut should not exceed the diameter of the shank.

To facilitate cutting in steps the three-position turret stop (see Fig. 7) is set by first lowering and locking the cutter against the face of the work. The depth of cut is then divided into equal steps (not exceeding the limits of the router or cutter) and the turret stop screws set accordingly, using the shortest screw for the final depth of cut, and setting the depth slide above the longest screw by an equal amount. Anti-vibration lock nuts are fitted to the screws and must be tightened to maintain the depth settings while the router is running. The cutter is plunged into the work and each step cut in sequence by rotating the turret to the next lower stop between each. If the required depth of cut is greater than obtainable in the three steps, lift the depth slide by an equal

amount and repeat the sequence. Heavy-duty routers are also fitted with a height stop to restrict the return lift (see Fig. 1). This can be used to set the maximum rise of the cutter when undercutting with a T-slot, edge-grooving cutter, or for other similar operations.

Sub-Bases

To maintain the cut square to the edge or face of the work the router must be supported on a level plane throughout the length of the cut. However, when edge-moulding or trimming the larger proportion of the router base is overhanging the edge of the work, resulting in a tendency to off-balance and tilt. To counteract this a wider sub-base should be used, such as a proprietary extension base, or a purpose-made one cut from flat sheet material (Fig. 8).

Stepped sub-bases are used to support the router when recessing wide areas (see Fig. 9) or to provide clearance for the projecting lip when trimming edge veneers or laminates (see page 97).

To avoid marking or scratching the sur-

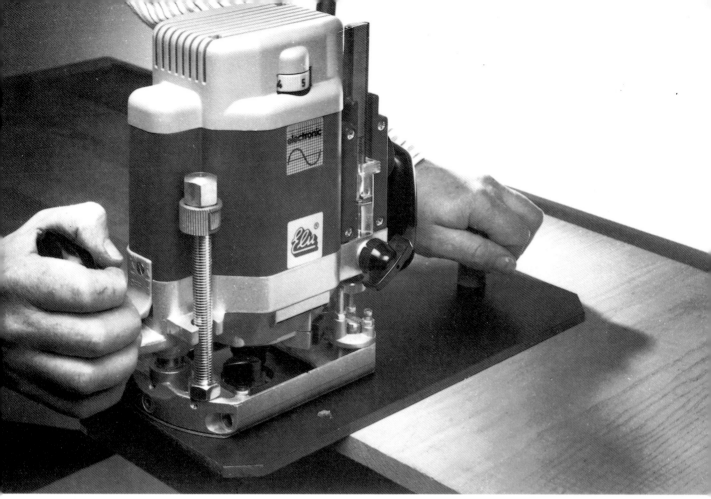

▲ FIG. 8 · ▼ FIG. 9

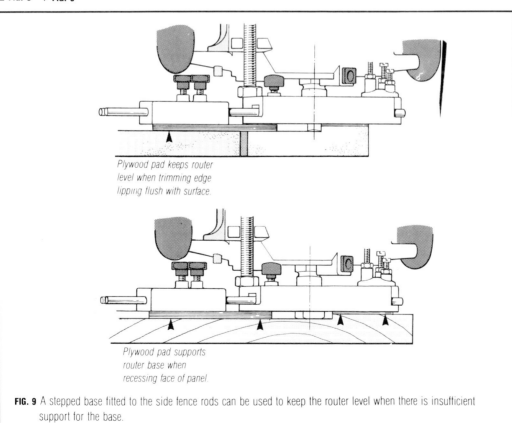

Plywood pad keeps router level when trimming edge lipping flush with surface.

Plywood pad supports router base when recessing face of panel.

ABOVE Fig. 8 When edge trimming or profiling, an extension base prevents the router from tipping keeping the cutter axis at right angles to the face of the work throughout the length of the cut.

FIG. 9 A stepped base fitted to the side fence rods can be used to keep the router level when there is insufficient support for the base.

face of the work, the underside of the plastic base must be kept clean, grease-free and perfectly smooth. Any scratching or burrs should be removed with fine wet and dry abrasive paper and polished with fine metal polish or cutting agent (as used on car paintwork). To protect highly finished or easily marred surfaces the base can be faced with felt held with double-sided tape.

To provide level support for the router when relief carving the face of a small or narrow workpiece, secure it to a flat surface (double-sided tape, folding wedges, etc.), and fasten levelling blocks or battens along each edge to form a flat plane with the highest surface of the work. During cutting, the router base spans between the blocks and top surface of the work, allowing the depth of cut to be set and varied as required. Where the router base is narrower than the

▲ FIG. 10   ▼ FIG. 11

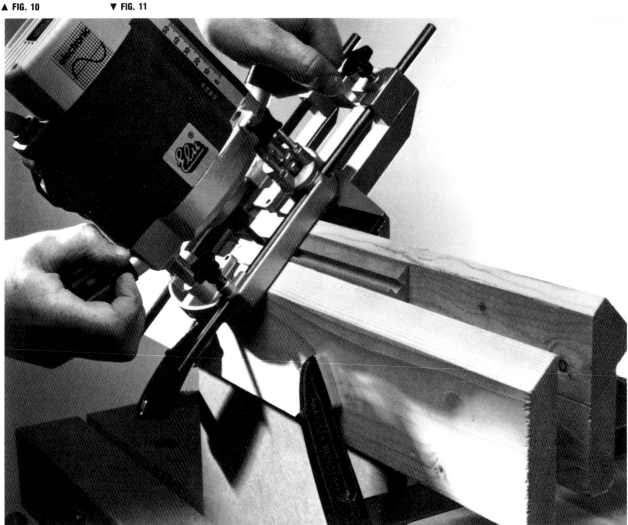

width between the higher surfaces, 'ski' bars can be fitted to increase the span (see Fig. 10). Similarly, when cutting mortises, grooves or mouldings along narrower edges, the support width for the router can be increased by clamping square-edged battens either side of the work. Use a try square to set the battens parallel and level to each other and ensure that clamps or other holding devices do not prevent the smooth continuous movement of the router. This latter method can also be used to support the router at an angle to the edge. The required angle is planed along the top edge of each batten and aligned either side of the workpiece using a bevel gauge (see Fig. 11).

Overcut Boards

There is also a tendency for the router to run out of line and tilt, both as it enters and leaves the workpiece. To prevent this, overcut boards should be fitted at either end of the cut both to provide a level plane for the router base to slide on and to extend the edge to keep the side fence in line. Overcut boards also prevent end grain (when crosscutting) or particle breakout at the end of the cut (see Fig. 12).

Routing Natural Timber

The router can be used to perform most woodworking operations on natural timber, its fast cutting speed leaving a clean smooth finish. However, as with hand tools and other portable and stationary machines, the problems of grain direction, variations in grain texture and end grain breakout must be taken into account and much in respect of the first two points will depend on the experience of the operator. End grain breakout and splitting can be prevented in one of several ways. The easiest is to leave the workpiece oversize to allow the router cut to overrun and trim off afterwards following the grain direction. Where this is not possible, overcut or extension pieces, as used to support the end grain when hand-planing, can be positioned at the start and end of the cut, with the faces set flush with those of the workpiece (see Fig. 12). Alternatively, when trimming panels each edge can be cut in

sequence, making all cuts across the grain first and removing the split corners when trimming the remaining edges with the grain direction (see Fig. 13).

Guiding the Router

Although the plunge router can be used effectively freehand to achieve both accurate and often highly creative work (see page 86), most precision machining operations are carried out with a fence or other form of guide.

Mouldings and other cuts made parallel to the edge of the workpiece can be worked with the aid of the side fence supplied with most machines. It can also be used when cutting housings across the face of a panel parallel to the edges or ends. However, the maximum dimension of the cut in from the edge of the work is restricted by the length of the side fence mounting rods. Longer rods can be substituted but should be limited to retain their rigidity.

When working across the face of a flat panel or board, the base of the router can be run against a straight edge secured across the work (see page 57). This method can be used not only to cut parallel to an edge but also when making parallel and angled cuts across the face of a panel.

By fitting a guide bush to the base of the router or by using a self-guiding cutter, the router can be used to follow a flat pattern or template to cut regular or irregular shapes. Templates are of particular use when carrying out repetitive operations or for batch production (see page 62).

Self-guiding cutters can also be used to follow the edge of the workpiece or material (see page 41). In this way mouldings and rebates can be cut precisely and evenly along straight or curved edges. Edges and edge laminates and veneers can also be trimmed using a flush self-guided cutter (see page 96).

One of the simplest methods of cutting regular curved or arched work is with a trammel bar or circle cutting guide, the router being swung round a single or related centre points to scribe an arc or multiradial curve (see page 75). A variation on the single-point trammel is the ellipse trammel

OPPOSITE ABOVE
Fig. 10 When recessing wide areas below the surface level of the material, the router can be supported on skis mounted on the side fence rods which then span across the reduced level.

OPPOSITE BELOW
Fig. 11 Bevel battens cut at a precise angle can be used to both mitre the ends of the material and to cut grooves to take a jointing tongue.

Safety Tip

When using the side fence or any other accessory check that all adjusting screws and clamps are tight before starting the initial cut, and frequently prior to subsequent passes. Some router manufacturers fit anti-vibration springs to the threaded thumbscrews. Ensure that the springs are in place.

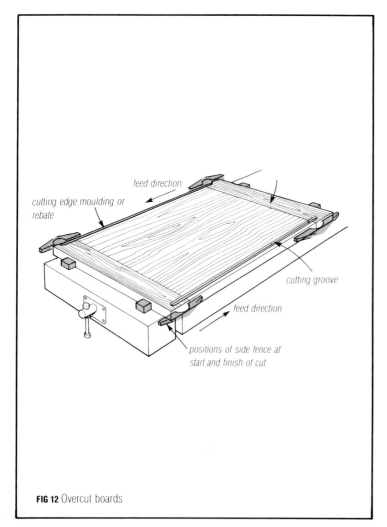

FIG 12 Overcut boards

▲ FIG. 12

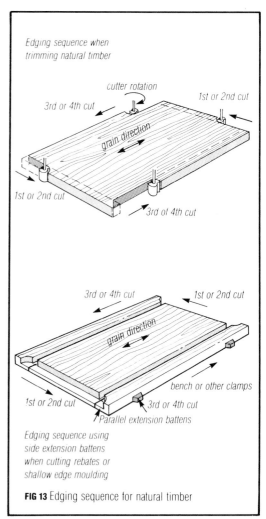

FIG 13 Edging sequence for natural timber

▲ FIG. 13

Safety Tip

Most routers have a simple slide switch that can be easily and inadvertently knocked on, so do check before plugging in that the router switch is in the 'off' position. Also check that the power cable is held away from the work (ideally lead over the shoulder or suspended from above) and that the work area is clear to allow easy and safe control of the router.

used to produce oval-shaped panels and mouldings (see page 75).

In many cutting operations the precise positioning of rebates, mortises and other cuts for joints, fittings and decorative features is of the utmost importance. For these purposes and for the repetitive production of matching components a jig to hold and position the work can be made up, often incorporating a template or guides to control the exact path of the router (see page 71).

Cutting With the Router
Direction of Cut

Whether using the router as a handheld or stationary machine for edge cutting or trimming, the direction of feed must always oppose the rotational direction of the cutter (see Fig. 14). If fed in the wrong direction the cutter will tend to throw the router away from the cutting face. When cutting across the face of the work (when cutting a groove or housing) the feed direction is unimportant. When cutting internal edges remember to feed the cutter in a clockwise direction, and for external edge profiling in the opposite or anticlockwise direction.

Feed Speeds

To maintain the life of your router, care should be taken not to overload the motor unduly, a clear sign of which is an immediate decrease in the speed and subsequently the noise of the motor. Therefore with a little experience the operator will be able to maintain an adequate and even feed speed relative to the work by the sound of the motor, a skill which will in time become fairly natural and automatic. A sure indication that the feed speed is dropping too low is if the cutter overheats, leaving burn marks on the face of the cut (see below). Burn marks are often apparent at the corners or change of angle in the line of the cut. This is due to the slight hesitation in the feed speed as the router changes direction. Burning can also occur at any point along the cut where it is necessary for the operator to change grip or to avoid an obstruction in the path of the router. Again this is due to hesitation and slowing of the feed speed. Always try to eliminate any possible obstructions before starting the cut and maintain a smooth steady feed during it. Also avoid stopping the router in the cut when you reach the end. If you cannot continue to feed the cutter out of the cut (when cutting stopped rebates, etc.), slide it away from the face of the cut or release the plunge lock to lift the cutter clear. For safety always release the plunge lock, switch off, and allow the speed to diminish before lifting the router off the work.

Cutter Speeds

The optimum cutting speed for a 3mm cutter to produce a clean cut with minimal cutter distress is 1,520 metres per minute, which represents a cutter speed of approximately 152,000 rpm. Similarly, a 12mm diameter cutter has an optimum speed of 38,000 rpm. But these speeds are well outside the range of the single-phase hand router with a maximum speed of 25,000 rpm. It is not until the cutter diameter reaches 19mm that the optimum speed matches the available router spindle speed. However, these optimum speeds are to some point impractical as many other factors such as variations in feed speed, the characteristics of the material being worked, and the type and profile of the cutter itself can drastically reduce the maintainable spindle speed under load. Also, the lower the input power of the router the more drastic will be the reduction in speed as the load increases. As the speed drops the quality of the finished cut will diminish while the temperature along the cutting edges will increase, causing cutter distress and possible burning of the workface.

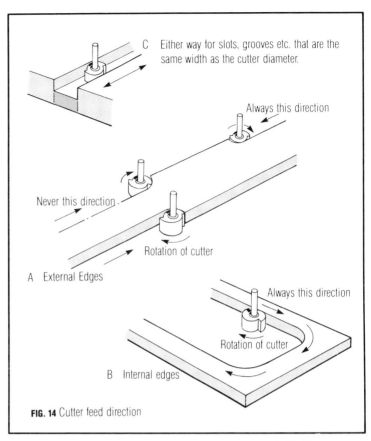

FIG. 14 Cutter feed direction

▲ FIG. 14

ROUTING SPEED CHART

With the introduction of electronic variable speed routers far greater control is available in selecting the most suitable speed to suit the application, material, and cutter. All speeds recommended in the following chart are no-load speeds and suggested only as an approximate guide.

Router Power (watts input)		600 to 800	1000 to 2000	600 to 800	1000 to 2000	600 to 800	1000 to 2000	600 to 800	1000 to 2000	600 to 800	1000 to 2000
Router Speed – RPM (no load)		8000		12000		16000		18000		24000	
Material	**Cutter diameter**	**Degree of Suitability**									
Softwood and low density hardwood	3 – 9mm / 12 – 32mm / 38 – 56mm										
Hardwoods or hard plastic with high melting point, MDF, Chipboard	3 – 9mm / 12 – 32mm / 32 – 56mm										
Soft and hard plastics with low melting point	3 – 9mm / 12 – 32mm / 38 – 56mm										
Routing aluminium**	3 – 9mm										
Drilling with the plunge router:											
Router drills, Counter sinks	3 – 12mm										
Hinge sinkers*	15 – 20mm / 25 – 35mm										

☐ AVOID   ◨ POSSIBLE   ■ GOOD   ☐ BEST

Note * Applies to special Trend tool for use in high speed router ** Refer to special cutters for duralium and UPVC extrusion

2 | Holding the Work

The method used to secure the work when routing depends mainly on the type of operation and the size of the workpiece or material. For many one-off or basic routing operations the traditional range of holding tools and devices can be utilized. But in more complex or repetitive operations fast-release systems such as vacuum clamping are generally more efficient and, once familiar and with the equipment available, can be adapted to suit the more basic operations or to develop new ones.

A poor finish is often the result of the inability to maintain a continuous and even feed rate, a common interruption being the need to stop and reposition clamps, wedges and other fastenings. It is therefore essential to plan carefully the method of holding the work and/or template and positioning any relevant stops or packing. Ensure that they are clear of the path of the body of the router and also that wingnuts, tommy bars and other parts are out of the path of the cutter beneath the work.

G-cramps and quick-action clamps of various sizes can be used for temporary clamping, especially when large areas of material are involved, clamps being positioned well clear of the cut line. Ensure that any overhang over the edge of the bench or table is supported on trestles or extension arms to keep the surface of the material flat and level as it is parted.

Sash cramps are commonly used to hold narrow rails by each end, the cramp itself being held in the bench vice. When using this method a block inserted beneath the rail or a pin or clamp fitted at one end should be

used to prevent it turning between the jaws (see Fig. 15).

Short thick battens and blocks can be easily held in the conventional woodworking bench vice, taking care to ensure that the cutter will clear between or above the vice jaws or face linings and that the under side of the router base is above the level of the bench surface. Do not attempt to hold thin battens sticking out either end of the vice as they may tend to bend under the weight of the router. Bench vices can also be used to secure clamping boards or bases fitted to the workpiece itself (where fastenings or glue marks are acceptable), a batten or block being fastened to the under side of the board and clamped between the vice jaws.

To avoid the need to clamp to the edge of the workbench or work surface, traditional bench dogs and holdfasts such as those fitted to the Sjoberg range of woodworking benches offer a secure method of holding the work clear of the path of the router.

In the same way over-centre or toggle clamps can be screwed to the surface of the bench or to a flat board secured over it, conveniently positioned to suit the shape of the workpiece (see Fig. 16). Over-centre clamps are particularly useful as they are quickly released and can be operated one-handed, making them ideal for use in conjunction with or incorporated into jigs and templates.

Another method of securing small panels to a flat surface is with folding wedges or eccentric cams, the latter being ideal for holding irregular-shaped work (see Fig. 17). To prevent wedges or cams being released in

⚠ **Safety Tip**

Never overload the router by cutting too deep in one pass. Never use blunt or damaged cutters and always feed the cutter into the work in the opposite direction to that of the rotation of the cutter. Use the correct type of cutter to suit the material and cutting operation. Always install the cutter correctly in the collet.

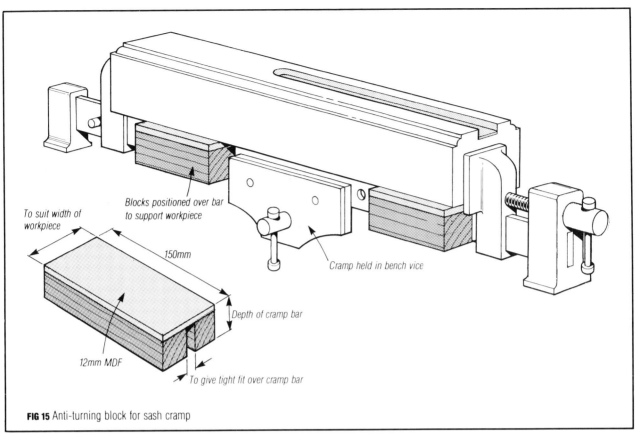

Blocks positioned over bar
to support workpiece

To suit width of
workpiece

150mm

Depth of cramp bar

12mm MDF

To give tight fit over cramp bar

Cramp held in bench vice

FIG 15 Anti-turning block for sash cramp

▲ **FIG. 15**   ▼ **FIG. 16**

use, fixed stops should be positioned along opposite edges or points round the workpiece. Wedges can be used either in pairs against a fixed stop or with one of the pair fastened and the other driven against it. When fitting eccentric cams the pivot point is drilled just off centre and a substantial screw or bolt fitted to resist the clamping pressure.

One method of particular use when clamping flat panels or templates is the use of double-sided tape or pads. Heavy-duty double-sided tapes such as carpet tape are best for this purpose, in particular those composed of a rubber-based adhesive. To ensure good adhesion all mating surfaces should have a smooth flat surface and be cleaned to remove any dust or grease. Porous baseboards, template and work-surface materials can be sealed with a quick-drying floor sealer or varnish for better adhesion. After use the surfaces can be gently prised apart and the remaining tape rolled off with the thumb. Stubborn adhesive tapes can generally be removed with lighter fluid without damage to the

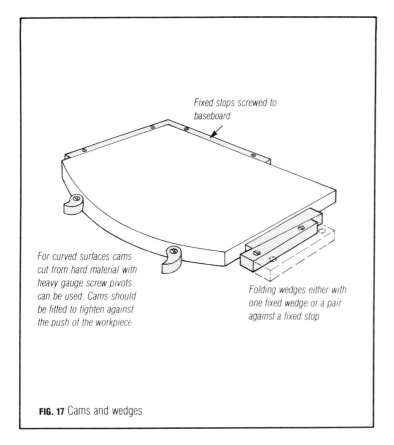

Fixed stops screwed to baseboard

For curved surfaces cams cut from hard material with heavy gauge screw pivots can be used. Cams should be fitted to tighten against the push of the workpiece

Folding wedges either with one fixed wedge or a pair against a fixed stop

FIG. 17 Cams and wedges

▲ **FIG. 17**

FIG. 18 ►

FIG. 18 Vacuum Chuck Construction

a, To ensure good cohesion, vacuum chucks must be constructed to provide both adequate vacuum feed and support for the workpiece to prevent it buckling under vacuum pressure. Only diagram (3) below shows the most effective principle of chuck construction the other methods (1) and (2) should be avoided.

(1) Inadequate support for thin workpiece material.

(2) Inadequate area of workpiece exposed to vacuum.

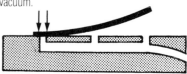

(3) Good vacuum area combined with adequate material support.

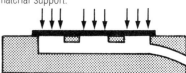

Vacuum Chuck Materials.

b, Wide self-adhesive strip can be cut into narrow strips or to produce shallow curved edges. The strip is between 2mm to 3mm thick closed cell neoprene material. Thicker material is not recommended as vibration or movement of the workpiece or template can result creating a poor edge finish. Reliable joints can be obtained by overlapping the ends of adjoining straps and cutting through both with a razor blade or scalpel.

c, Neoprene vacuum ring seals are available in various diameters for chuck construction generally from 12mm × 12mm and 14mm × 12mm section (Trend supply them in 150mm and 200mm diameter respectively). The rings should be set into a recess approximately half the thickness of the ring material routered into the face of the chuck.

surface, but do check on a concealed area or offcut first. When sticking templates to a workpiece use only thin double-sided tape, not the thicker foam pads, which give slightly and allow some movement between the two surfaces.

Vacuum Clamping

Although more commonly used in industrial workshops involved in fast repetitive batch work, vacuum clamping can be just as easily applied to one-off or short production runs in smaller craft or amateur workshops. In either case it is an efficient and effective method of holding both the workpiece and/or the template to each other or to the machine table.

The principle of vacuum clamping is simple. A suction chamber or chuck is produced using neoprene sealing strip to form an enclosed area slightly smaller than the area of the workpiece or template. The work is then laid over the chuck and the air between them is removed by a vacuum pump. The suction between the d, Self-adhesive neoprene sheet should be between 1.5mm and 2.5mm thick. One method of cutting the sheet to size for pin-routing is to first fix the template to the underside of the chuck sub-base and apply the neoprene sheet to the top-side of the workframe after peeling away the protective backing. With the overhead mounted straight cutter set to cut through the neoprene sheet and minimally (no more than 1mm) into the face of the work frame trim the outer edge of the sheet by following the template outline. With a scalpel cut the inner edge of the seal leaving an adequate chuck area with the extract vent within it. Be sure to peel away the unwanted neoprene sheet before the adhesive reaches its full cohesive strength, a matter of a few hours.

d, Sheet sealant material for vacuum

e & f, While neoprene strip and sheet materials are stuck directly to the surface of the chuck, neoprene ring seals and round strip are set into a groove routered into the face or an upstand frame. Round neoprene sealing strip, much preferred by the furniture industry due to its flexibility, is generally available in 6mm and 8mm diameters and sold by the metre. It is best set into a chamferred groove (as with other inset strips) which grips the seal but also allows it room to compress reducing the gap between the chuck surface and the underside of the workpiece.

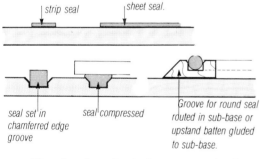

strip seal *sheet seal.*

seal set in chamferred edge groove *seal compressed* *Groove for round seal routed in sub-base or upstand batten glued to sub-base.*

g, Where the volume of work allows, a vacuum bench can be built incorporating horizontal and vertical face vacuum chucks and housing the vacuum pump, power sockets, isolating switches and foot operated vacuum control.

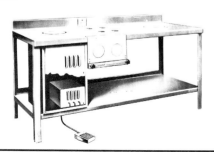

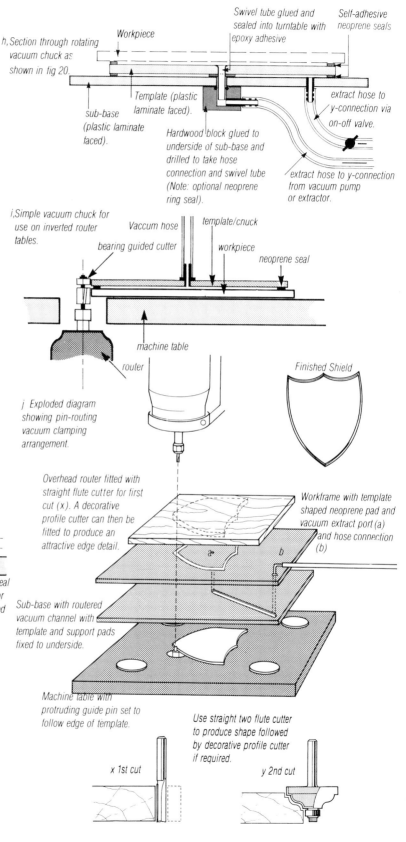

h, Section through rotating vacuum chuck as shown in fig 20.

Workpiece

Swivel tube glued and sealed into turntable with epoxy adhesive

Self-adhesive neoprene seals

Template (plastic laminate faced).

sub-base (plastic laminate faced).

Hardwood block glued to underside of sub-base and drilled to take hose connection and swivel tube (Note: optional neoprene ring seal).

extract hose to y-connection via on-off valve.

extract hose to y-connection from vacuum pump or extractor.

i, Simple vacuum chuck for use on inverted router tables.

Vaccum hose

bearing guided cutter

template/cnuck

workpiece

neoprene seal

machine table

router

Finished Shield

j Exploded diagram showing pin-routing vacuum clamping arrangement.

Overhead router fitted with straight flute cutter for first cut (x). A decorative profile cutter can then be fitted to produce an attractive edge detail.

Workframe with template shaped neoprene pad and vacuum extract port (a) and hose connection (b)

Sub-base with routered vacuum channel with template and support pads fixed to underside.

Machine table with protruding guide pin set to follow edge of template.

Use straight two flute cutter to produce shape followed by decorative profile cutter if required.

x 1st cut *y 2nd cut*

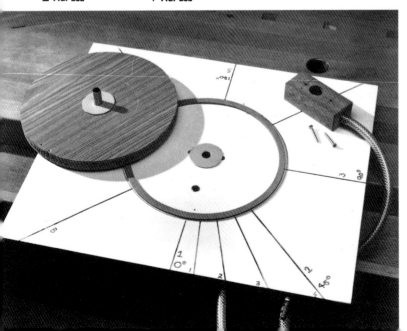

surfaces holds the components securely together.

The neoprene sealing strip can either be of the self-adhesive type applied direct to a flat clean surface (sheet materials faced with plastic laminate are best for this purpose), or it can be set slightly proud of the surface into a routered groove (see Fig. 18). Neoprene sealing strip should be of the closed-cell variety, self-adhesive strip or pad being between 1·5 and 2·5mm thick with a similar dimension left proud when insetting sealing strip. Do not use a thicker seal than this as vibration can arise, resulting in a poor finish; or, when holding templates, slight movement between the template and work-piece may occur. Neoprene tape and strip is available in various widths as well as a sheet pad material, which is particularly useful for cutting into either thin strips or shaped pads to suit the outer contour of the work. Once applied, neoprene pad material can be easily cut with the router using a small-diameter straight cutter. Prior to applying the tape ensure that surfaces are clean and dust-free. Ensure that there are no gaps in the seal by overlapping the tape at joints. Silicon seal-ant (as used to seal round baths and basins) can be used to seal most leaks and itself can be used to form a seal on small vacuum chucks.

For most routing purposes involving vacuum clamping surfaces up to a combined area of approximately 600 × 300mm, a small vacuum pump capable of producing about 17 psi is adequate and not too expensive. Alternatively, a commercial vacuum extractor can be used (see Fig. 4 page 13). In each case the vacuum extraction unit is connected via small-bore plastic tube and threaded hose connector (0·125 to 0·25 BSP) or standard-size HVLV dust extraction hose into the vacuum chamber. The exhaust port can be situated anywhere within the sealed chamber. Soft timber-based materials can be simply drilled slightly undersized and the fitting screwed in to cut its own thread but harder plastic will need to be threaded to ensure a secure connection. Leaking or loose fittings can often be refitted by the use of an epoxy adhesive, epoxy resin filler, or a silicon sealant. On and off switching is most conveniently operated by a foot switch, leaving both hands free to control the work.

To obtain maximum holding power the surface area exposed to the vacuum within the chamber should be as large as possible. However, the effect of the vacuum may be to pull and bow thin materials unless they are supported, and small support pads of the neoprene tape should be arranged within the chamber. The vacuum hose entry can be made at any convenient position within the chuck area.

Vacuum chucks can be used in several different ways to hold the workpiece on the machine table or baseboard, to hold the workpiece and template to a surface, or to hold the template above or below the workpiece (see Fig. 18).

Pin-Routing Application

When pin-routing beneath the overhead router it is advisable to mount the workpiece and template on a carrier frame. Fitted with handles either side, the frame allows easy and safe control of the work. By converting the carrier into a vacuum chuck the workpiece can be easily and quickly fitted to the carrier, leaving an unobstructed path for the cutter. The template is permanently held to the under side of the carrier by glue or double-sided tape.

Holding the Workpiece to a Flat Surface

Vacuum can also be used to hold the workpiece to a flat work surface or machining table. For this the sealing strip is applied to the table surface and an exhaust port drilled either from the edge or in the under side.

Universal Chucks

Rectangular and circular, single or double-faced vacuum chucks are suited to many general routing applications and it is well worth while making up a range of various sizes and shapes (see Fig. 19). These can be used for holding the workpiece to a work surface or to a template. Being less prone to damage, inset sealing strip is best suited for chucks intended for repetitive use. Avoid excessive overhang of the template or workpiece to avoid any tendency for excess leverage to tilt or pull the surfaces apart during the cutting operation. For batch work or complex shapes, vacuum chucks made up to match the workpiece contour are to be preferred. The template itself can be used to form the chuck – drilled to take the hose connection with the sealing strip applied to the reverse side. Although more straight-forward, this is most suited for work cut on the inverted router table, where the top-mounted vacuum hose will not interrupt the continuous path of the cutter.

Turntable Vacuum Chuck

This is a useful accessory for holding small panels when trimming or moulding along each edge. Since the split vacuum exhaust allows the workpiece to be turned without being released from the table. When trimming the edges of natural wood panels, this system allows the correct trimming sequence to avoid corner grain breakout to be quickly carried out. An indexing system can also be incorporated to facilitate the cutting of evenly spaced features around the circumference or across the face of the work (see Figs 18, 20a and b).

3 Cutters

Much of the versatility offered by modern routers results from the comprehensive range of cutters now available, allowing the user to select not only a cutter to produce a specific profile, but one that will give optimum performance between cutter durability and quality of surface finish, in relation to the material being worked, the machining operation being performed, and the economics of the job in hand.

To provide these options manufacturers' research has produced many developments in cutter construction techniques, in the composition of the materials from which they are made, in the methods of reinforcing the cutting edges for greater durability, and in the geometry of the cutting action.

Of these the most commonly used cutters, both in professional and amateur workshops, are of the tungsten carbide tipped type, which, although producing an inferior surface finish, are far more durable than the less expensive high-speed steel cutters and will handle a more varied range of materials, including those containing abrasive substances such as resin-based glues used in the manufacture of man-made particle and laminated boards.

However, it is not purely the abrasive nature of a material that can cause a cutting edge to dull. Being an excellent insulating material, wood tends to retain the frictional heat created by a rotating cutter (unlike metals, which tend to dissipate it). The temperature along the cutting edge can build up high enough not only to burn the wood but to change the temper and struc-

ture of the cutter metal. Therefore, for working particularly hard materials such as dense timbers and surface-coated metals, and even for detailing on fine-grained stone and marbles, various steel alloys as well as ceramic compositions and special coatings such as diamond crystals are now available or under development.

Cutter Materials

When selecting a cutter the quality of the metal from which it is made is, of course, all-important. Super high-speed steel (HSSE) grades of tool steels contain higher percentages of carbide, chromium and other metals (the actual content being a closely guarded secret by each rival manufacturer) than ordinary high-speed steels (HSS), best-quality HSS containing around 18% tungsten, 4·25% chromium, 1·1% vanadium and 0·75% carbon (it is interesting to note that American manufacturers are now replacing some of the tungsten content with molybdenum, an even harder and more durable metal). In the formation of tungsten carbide tooling cobalt, a softer metal, is used as a binder to hold the tungsten carbide grains together. In best-quality tungsten carbide steels ultrafine tungsten carbide grains are used, enabling the percentage of the softer cobalt binder to be reduced without increasing the brittleness of the tool.

But without actually taking samples of the cutter metal and subjecting it to laboratory tests it is virtually impossible for the end user to judge the quality of the cutter metal and he must rely on experience or the reputation of the better known manufacturers and suppliers.

When purchasing cutters, however, there are several points that can be checked which will give some indication of their quality.

Check that the shank is unpitted and evenly ground, and that there are no chips along the cutting edge. On TCT cutters check that the brazing has no voids, that the tips are supported at the end of the cutter, and that they have a polished finish. A rough finish indicates a cheap finishing process or no finishing at all. However, a slight even matt finish along the shank of some cutters is purposely applied to give better grip in the collet: this is often referred to as vapour blasting.

Stamp Sheet Steel
Stamped from sheet steel, these cutters – available in a range of straight, decorative and fixed-pin pilot cutters – are aimed at the DIY market as an economic alternative to HSS cutters (see Fig. 21). This method of manufacture does not allow for precise or specific cutting geometry to be achieved and the cutters can be easily bent out of line. However, the heat-treated steel retains a keen edge well and the hollow pilot pins are claimed to run cooler than solid pins. They are most suitable for infrequent use on soft non-abrasive materials such as softwoods and soft plastics. These cutters are generally considered to be disposable once they have deteriorated to the point where they need regrinding, but can be kept sharp during their life by occasional honing on their flat inside face.

High-Speed Steel (HSS)
HSS cutters can be sharpened to a far keener edge than the more durable tungsten carbide tipped (TCT) or solid carbide cutters, and will therefore produce a superior surface finish on non-abrasive materials if kept sharp by regular honing. Until recently, solid ground cutters (HSS, HSSE and SC) were generally ground with a curved cross-sectional flute. Most solid cutters are now ground with an angled flute similar to the angled flute of a tipped cutter, providing more efficient chip clearance (see Fig. 22).

▲ FIG. 21

ABOVE Fig. 21 Offered as an economical alternative to solid ground cutters, stamped steel sheet cutters are available in various straight and decorative profiles for use in low power routers.

Any excessive overheating will quickly result in fast deterioration of the cutting edges of HSS cutters, which may be impossible to restore. This can be avoided by keeping cutters sharp and maintaining a suitable feed speed for the material being worked (see page 23).

Super High-Speed Steel (HSSE)
Made of high-grade tool steels, these cutters have been developed in particular for the aluminium window industry to withstand the abrasive nature of anodized aluminium. They are also ideal for machining and fine engraving on dense hardwoods requiring a high-quality finish (see Fig. 23).

Tungsten Carbide Tipped (TCT)
Generally used for machining most types of wood and plastics, the tungsten carbide tips retain their cutting edge well even when used on hard abrasive materials. However, tungsten carbide is a brittle metal and cutting edges can be easily chipped if carelessly stored and handled. The tips or cutting edges consist of thin sections of

OVERLEAF Fig. 22 For fine detailing work on hardwoods high speed steel (HSS) or super high speed (HSSE) cutters produce a far superior finish to the more durable tungsten carbide tipped (TCT) cutters.

OVERLEAF Fig. 24 The durability of TCT cutters makes them essential for continuous production operations and offers a worthwhile alternative for the home craftsperson in spite of the extra capital outlay.

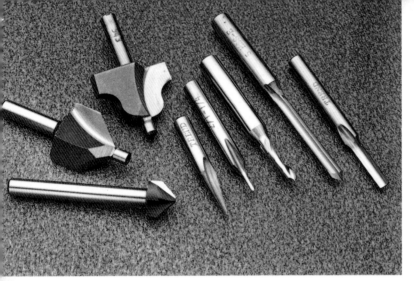

▲ FIG. 22

▲ FIG. 24

OPPOSITE Fig. 23
a HSSE cutters are
intended for machining
soft metals particularly
profiles having hard
anodised surfaces where
cutter durability and
standard of finish are
equally important.
b Standard routers fitted
with HSSE cutters can
be easily incorporated
in industrial jigs for
machining precision
components.

⚠ Safety Tip

Always wear eye
protection when
using tipped cutters.
Even the best quality
can occasionally
lose a tip.

---

tungsten carbide brazed on to heat treated tool steel ground to the flute configuration. The cost of TCT cutters is possibly two or three times that of HSS cutters of similar size, but both the time and cost saved on regrinding and replacement generally more than offset the initial extra outlay. If the quality of finish is of particular importance, when undertaking long production runs it may be worth considering using a matched pair of cutters, a TCT cutter, to remove the waste and a HSS cutter to make a final fine skimming cut (see Fig. 24).

Disposable-Tip Cutters

A fairly recent introduction is disposable-tip cutting tools, which use flat tungsten carbide or HSS blades held in place by a small hexagon-socket-headed screw. Each blade has a cutting edge ground on two edges (often four on square blades). As each edge dulls the blade is reversed or replaced,

saving on either resharpening or complete tool replacement. A major advantage is that the cutter can be effectively resharpened without removing it from the collet, eliminating the need to reset the machine (depth of cut, etc.) (see Fig. 25).

Solid Tungsten Carbide (SC)

Solid tungsten carbide cutters have the durability of TCT cutters but are less prone to failure, being machined from solid metal rather than having the tips brazed on. For this reason they are far safer as the 'tips' cannot become detached and fly off. Also, being machined from solid metal, they can be ground to produce a far superior plunge-cutting action than is possible with tipped cutters, and they can be used for applications where cutting temperatures are likely to be unavoidably higher than recommended for tipped cutters. While small-diameter cutters are only a little more expensive than tipped ones of similar size, the cost of larger sizes, from about 10mm diameter, is considerably higher.

Diamond Bonded

Diamond crystals are bonded under intense heat and pressure to the cutting faces to produce a very sharp and extremely durable cutting edge which leaves a fine surface finish.

Ceramic

Cutters manufactured from reinforced composite ceramic materials are now under development. They are claimed to be far more durable than carbide cutters and can withstand far higher working temperatures. As yet these are not generally available in the United Kingdom.

Cutter Design

Cutters differ not only in the material they are made of but in their geometry – that is, the configuration of the flutes, the angle at which the cutting edge or edges attack the material, and the way in which the cutter clears the swarf, chips or dust from the cut. The combination of these criteria determines the optimum speed at which the cutter can be fed into the material, the

▲ FIG. 23a · ▼ FIG. 23b

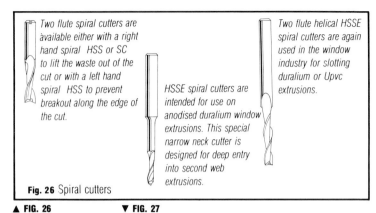

Two flute spiral cutters are available either with a right hand spiral HSS or SC to lift the waste out of the cut or with a left hand spiral HSS to prevent breakout along the edge of the cut.

HSSE spiral cutters are intended for use on anodised duralium window extrusions. This special narrow neck cutter is designed for deep entry into second web extrusions.

Two flute helical HSSE spiral cutters are again used in the window industry for slotting duralium or Upvc extrusions.

Fig. 26 Spiral cutters

▲ FIG. 26   ▼ FIG. 27

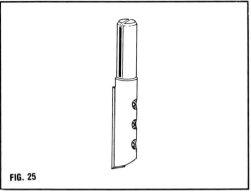

FIG. 25

▲ FIG. 25

ABOVE RIGHT Fig. 25 Disposable blade cutters allow the cutter to be effectively resharpened without removing the cutter from the collet and disturbing the machine setting.

ABOVE LEFT Fig. 27 Burrs, end cut burrs, two flute, single flute, and spiral cutters, are available in most cutter materials, those shown being machined from solid carbide.

amount of material that can be removed on each rotation of the cutter, and the quality of the finished surface.

The most common configurations are straight cut, helical spirals, shear cut, and rasps or burrs, each with its own variations (see Figs 26 and 27).

Straight Cutters

Single Flute

Small-diameter single-flute cutters are used for fast cutting, a feed speed of up to 6 metres per minute being possible in wood-based materials (10 metres per minute obtainable on CNC machines). These are generally described as eccentric cutters with their single flutes ground offset to the round shanks. This allows clearance between the back of the cutter and the face of the material (see Fig. 30). Concentric single-flute cutters (generally referred to as spoon bits), which are in themselves ground concentric,

are designed for use in an eccentric chuck as used on overhead routing machines (see page 45). While concentric cutters can be used in an eccentric chuck (Fig. 28), because of the lack of radial clearance spoon bits should not be used in the normal concentric collet of a handheld or stationary router.

Two Flute

Two-flute cutters require a far slower feed speed of about 1–2 metres per minute (5 metres per minute obtainable on CNC machines). They produce a far better surface finish than single-flute and are generally preferred for cutting abrasive or hard materials. Most two-flute cutters are now supplied with bottom cut – that is, tipped or ground cutting edges on the end of the cutter – to facilitate plunge cutting.

Spiral Cut:

Up-cut Spirals

For square-edge work, cutting housing, slots and grooves, many woodworkers prefer to use helical-cut spiral cutters which cut with a continuous shearing action, leaving a smoother surface than the intermittent impact of a straight-flute cutter. Also, they tend to lift the waste material out of the cut rather than packing it around and increasing friction on the cutter, as can happen with straight-flute cutters. Spiral cutters are of particular use when machining timbers with varying grain directions, their cutting action slicing through the fibres rather than tearing at them.

Helical spiral flutes, which are effectively an elongated shear angle, are more commonly used on plastics and aluminium, which require even better chip clearance

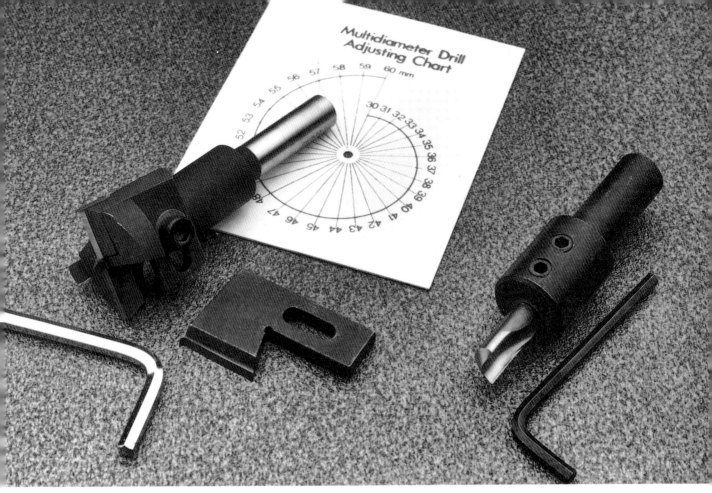

ABOVE Fig. 28 Spoon bits (right) designed for use in eccentric machine chucks allow a degree of kerf width adjustment. Adjustable blade cutters offer larger cutting diameters but are restricted to cutting speeds of 4000 RPM or less.

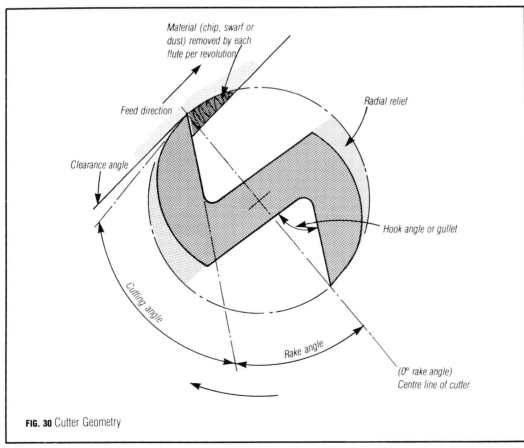

Material (chip, swarf or dust) removed by each flute per revolution

Feed direction

Radial relief

Clearance angle

Hook angle or gullet

Cutting angle

Rake angle

(0° rake angle)
Centre line of cutter

FIG. 30 Cutter Geometry

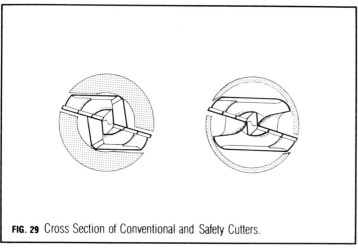

FIG. 29 Cross Section of Conventional and Safety Cutters.

▲ **FIG. 29**

than wood since any swarf remaining close to the cutting edge increases frictional heat, often fusing itself into one mass, which causes excessive heat to build up along the cutting edges.

Down-cut Spirals
Although not as commonly used as up-cut spirals, down-cut spirals can be effective when working with the router inverted (as a spindle moulder), the waste being lifted up out of the cut instead of falling back into the air intake slots in the router motor housing (a common cause of router failure). When used with the router above the work it is necessary to ensure adequate clearance directly beneath the cut to allow the waste to fall away.

Shear Cut
Most decorative-profile cutters are ground with the cutting edge angled at about 5° to produce a slight shear or slicing action to reduce breakout along the edge of the cut and improve the quality of finish (see Fig. 33). This action is particularly useful when working timbers with varying grain directions or areas of end grain.

Rasps and Burrs
Rasps and burrs are available in a variety of shapes as well as straight cutters with either drill-point or bottom-cut ends for plunge-cutting. Ground from solid carbide, they are mainly used for cutting glass reinforced plastics and removing burrs on metal. They can also be used for shaping or carving wood and for edge

finishing or for cutting pierced apertures in metals such as soft grades of aluminium.

Safety Cutters
Some cutters, in particular decorative-profile cutters, are purposely ground with a limited depth of cut. This is achieved by grinding away only part of the flute metal behind the cutting edge, limiting the distance that the cutting edge can cut into the material before the back of the cutter rubs on the face. The depth of cut is generally restricted to about 1·5mm, which is ideally suited to edge-moulding operations, the cut being made in several passes, increasing the depth of the cutter on each and finishing with a final skimming cut to the full depth of the profile (see Fig. 29).

Cutter Geometry

The same basic geometry applies to router cutters as to any other rotating cutter, the cutting force being delivered by the top face of the cutting edge over an area equal to the depth of cut (the amount by which the cutter is immersed in the workpiece). This exerts a shear force along a plane extending from the extreme tip of the cutting edge, freeing and carrying the chip clear. The result of the force exerted during the shearing action and the friction created by the chip clearing across the face of the cutter appearing as heat along the cutting edge.

By decreasing the angle at which the cutting face approaches the material (by increasing the rake angle – see Fig. 30) the force required for a given feed speed and depth of cut is reduced, producing a cleaner and cooler cutting action. However, the smaller the cutting angle becomes, the thinner and weaker the flute becomes. It is therefore necessary to maintain an optimum angle as a compromise between the two. To simplify their profile grinding and facilitate their construction, some cutters have a rake angle of 0°, producing a scraping action which, though not leaving such a clean finish as a positive rake angle, is ideal for working timbers that tend to split and tear out easily.

To eliminate unnecessary friction, only the cutting face should come into contact

---

⚠ Safety Tip

Try to avoid being interrupted while working. Warn other people and particularly children beforehand to keep well away until you have finished. However, even though most of your concentration will be on what you are doing with the router, remain aware of what is going on around you to avoid being shocked by something unexpected into making a mistake or causing an accident.

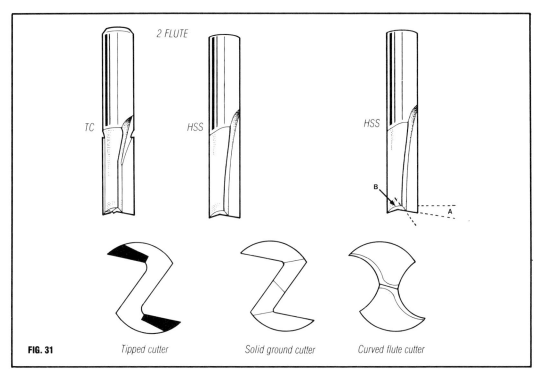

LEFT Fig. 31
Irrespective of whether a
TCT cutter has a centre
tip, a slight lead-in on
the base of each flute of
3° is recommended (A)
with the back of the
cutting edge ground to a
minimum angle of
5° (B).

FIG. 31   Tipped cutter   Solid ground cutter   Curved flute cutter

▲ FIG. 31

with the material being cut, while the waste material must be cleared away from the face as quickly as possible (see Fig. 30).

To provide clearance or radial relief between the outer surface of the cutter and the material being cut, in order to eliminate friction between the two and encourage swarf to clear freely, each flute is ground away behind the tip of the cutting edge in an eccentric curve (generally at an angle of not less than 15°). On some TCT cutters (deep-mortise staggered-tooth cutters, for instance) the cutter is ground concentric and the clearance ground only on the cutting edge of the TC tip, which is then left slightly proud to give further clearance behind it. Small-diameter cutters often suffer from lack of clearance behind the cutting edge as to grind them sufficiently would make them weak. When using these take care to prevent swarf and resin building up behind the cutting edge, which reduces the clearance further. Cutters specifically designed for cutting plastics tend to have greater clearance behind the cutting edge to prevent weld-back – the swarf welding itself back into the kerf (cut) with frictional heat from the cutter.

The hook angle – that is, the angle formed within the gullet – should be as open as possible to allow swarf to clear quickly and cleanly. The faster it clears the faster the cutter can be fed in to the material. Plastics generally require a flatter hook angle than timber to obtain a good finish.

Most cutters generally used for cutting wood are either single- or two-flute, although multi-bladed tools are available for use on specific materials or when limitations on feed or cutting speeds occur. Although, theoretically, increasing the number of cutting edges should produce better results for a given feed speed, practical limitations occur with insufficient gullet room, particularly with small-diameter cutters, unable to accommodate the waste material, which soon causes the cutter to choke up. Other factors which affect good cutter design are perfect roundness of the shank and its precise alignment along the length of the cutter to eliminate whip and ensure vibration-free running mirror-polished cutter faces to give fast waste clearance and avoid the build-up of resin deposits, and sharpness and perfect centring of the centre tip and end cutters to ensure clean plunge-cutting with no eccentric movement to cause ovality in the hole.

When plunge cutting holes up to 8mm diameter at 90°, a centre-tipped TCT cutter is

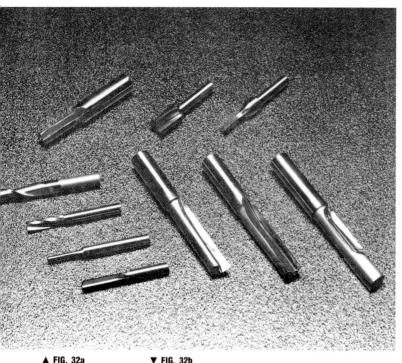

ABOVE Fig. 32a Straight cutters are available in all materials in a wide range of sizes, shank diameters and lengths. Single-flute cutters give a fast feed rate while two-flute or spiral flute cutters produce a superior finish.

RIGHT Fig. 32b Recent developments in cutter design have led to the introduction of shear fluted straight cutters having a minimal lefthand spiral producing a slicing action to prevent breakout on the top edge of the work.

▼ **FIG. 32b**

ing as easily, will stay cooler and retain its edge longer. As a general guide cutters of 8mm diameter and above should have centre tips if frequent plunge entry is envisaged, but below this size the better chip clearance capability of untipped cutters is to be preferred. Because of the difficulty the cutter has in clearing swarf from beneath it, particularly when plunge-cutting or routing enclosed housings and grooves, the end-cut geometry has to be fairly precise, providing adequate clearance and hook angles.

The centrifugal force generated by a cutter revolving at router cutting speeds is extremely high and the slightest imbalance in the cutter can cause vibration to set up, which results in a poor surface finish and damage to both the cutter and the router bearings. Manufacturers of good-quality cutters can generally be relied upon to ensure the correct balance in the design and production of their cutters when new. However, it is necessary to take care to maintain that balance throughout its life by careful resharpening and regrinding (see Cutter Maintenance, page 121).

When machining resinous timbers friction can be reduced considerably by using either teflon-coated cutters – an anti-stick coating more commonly used on frying pans and saw blades, which reduces friction and prevents resins and other adhesive substances sticking to its surface – or PTFE dry lubricant spray, which performs the same function but is more convenient, being applied as needed by aerosol spray to cutters, machine slides or lead screws.

Cutter Types

Straight Cutters
Straight cutters for making straight-sided cuts (that is, at 90° to the base of the router) are available in all flute types in a wide range of cutter lengths and diameters. Single- and double-flute cutters are generally used for cutting grooves, rebates and slots, for panel cutting and for square-edge trimming, although some are designed for specific jobs – for example, staggered-tooth cutters are for deep slot mortising, and hinge-recessing cutters are for shallow lateral mortising (see Fig. 32).

not generally necessary. Above this size, however, centre-tipped TCT cutters will drill holes more efficiently. However, when transversing the cut, having plunged into the material, the centre tip can allow resin and swarf to lodge, increasing the friction on the end of the cutter. Alternatively, an untipped cutter with good angular clearance (see Fig. 31), although not plung-

▲ **FIG. 33**

LEFT Fig. 33 Self-guiding cutters are generally used for edge trimming operations such as rebating and decorative moulding. Bearing pilots having a ball race fitted to the shank or end pin are less likely to burn the workpiece.

Most straight cutters are now produced with the end cut suitably ground for plunge cutting, but drill-point cutters, more suited to continuous drilling to the detriment of their chip clearance ability, can be obtained in a limited range of sizes.

Decorative-Profile Cutters

These are available in a wide range of profiles, including classic mouldings such as ovolo and ogee as well as rounding over, bead, chamfer, cove, and V-groove cutters. Self-guided cutters, either with fixed-pin or ball-bearing pilots, as well as un-guided for use with guide bushes or machine fences, are used to produce decorative edges and panel mouldings, either repeating the complete cutter profile or for multi-cutting – that is, making up more complex mouldings repeating the same or part of the profile or in combination with other cutters. Many bearing guided cutters are now supplied with alternative diameter bearings, allowing the user the choice of width of moulding (see Fig. 33 and the Profile Guide on page 126).

Decorative-moulding cutters are also available in the form of scribing sets consisting of either one or a pair of cutters, which allow the profile and its reverse to be cut to form scribed joints in door, window and other types of frame construction (see Fig. 34).

Special-Purpose Cutters

Many cutters are produced to perform a specific job, ranging from simple edge rebating to more precise operations such as cutting dovetails, T-slots and mitre joints (see page 106). They are designed to minimize the setting-up and cutting time, as well as to ensure a high degree of accuracy. As with scribing cutters, matched sets of cutters are often used to cut joint profiles such as tongue and groove and rule joints, one cutter machining the joint profile, the other cutting the precise reverse profile to fit into it. Profiles for fitting door furniture and building components can also be machined by special cutters. These include hinge sinkers for fitting concealed cabinet hinges, library-shelving-strip double-rebate cutters and capillary groove and weather seal cutters for door and window manufacture (see page 164). A cutter of particular interest is the finger joint cutter, designed for end-jointing dense timbers by providing a long glue line for exceptional strength (see page 112).

Trimming Cutters

A comprehensive range of laminate trimmers allows most edge-finishing operations that may occur in the construction or fitting of plastic-laminate-faced worktops, furni-

⚠ Safety Tip

Because of the extremely high peripheral speed of large diameter cutters such as the fielded panel type, they cannot safely be used in a hand-held router. They should only be used in table or overhead mounted stationary machines.

RIGHT Fig. 34
Scribing cutters,
available as a matched
pair or as a single
arbor assembly,
simultaneously machine
the decorative moulding
and panel groove along
the stile/rail edge and
cut the reverse moulding
on the rail ends.

▲ **FIG. 34**

RIGHT Fig. 35a   Multi-
bladed cutters for edge
moulding, grooving and
rebating can be
assembled using plain
or threaded shank
arbors. In this way
specific profiles can be
achieved using various
diameter and thickness
cutters.

▲ **FIG. 35a** · ▼ **FIG. 36**

RIGHT Fig. 36   One
specific use of end-
threaded arbors is for
machining grooves
within a pre-cut rebate
to accommodate
proprietary weather and
smoke seal profiles.

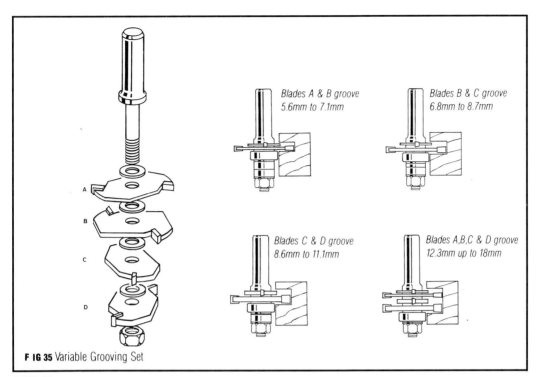

F IG 35 Variable Grooving Set

Blades A & B groove
5.6mm to 7.1mm

Blades B & C groove
6.8mm to 8.7mm

Blades C & D groove
8.6mm to 11.1mm

Blades A,B,C & D groove
12.3mm up to 18mm

LEFT Fig. 35b Four typical grooving cutter combinations are shown, the quad groover being assembled from grooving cutters ranging from 3·2mm to 18mm. Depth of cut is set using 6·8mm, 8·8mm, or 12·8m diameter guide bearings.

▲ FIG. 35b

ture and fittings to be quickly carried out, leaving a precise unchipped finish. Both self- and non-guided cutters are available for producing square (90°) and bevel (30°, 45°, 60° and 80°) edges. For cutting apertures to accept hobs, sinks and other inset fittings pierce-and-trim cutters are designed to follow a pre-cut opening beneath the laminate (see page 103).

Slotting and Grooving Cutters

The use of slotting, grooving and slitting blades fitted to a threaded arbor enables the woodworker to assemble multiple-bladed cutters to his own specification using spacers and shims to determine precisely the width of each groove, tongue, or rebate, and set the depth by the outer diameter of the cutters themselves. For flush cutting, threaded groovers fitted to a threaded arbor eliminate any protrusion beneath the blade, allowing slots to be cut into a rebate flush with its lower surface. The cutter is guided by the router's side fence, a guide disc, or a bearing race, the depth of cut then being governed by the bearing's outer diameter. When assembling arbors the guide bearings and cutters should always be fitted at the top of the threaded arbor as close to the shank as

possible to minimize the risk of vibration (see Figs 35 and 36).

Self-Guiding Cutters

Some router cutters are designed to guide themselves either by means of a fixed pilot pin machined as part of the cutter shank or with a ball-bearing race fitted to the end or to the shank of the cutter (see Fig. 33). The pin diameter on fixed-pin cutters leaves a much smaller corner radius than is possible with a bearing guide, but they are more likely to overheat and leave burn marks on the workpiece. Most bearing pilot cutters can be fitted with bearings of various diameters to alter the effective width of the cutting edge and so change the cutter profile. This is particularly useful on rebate cutters, the same cutter being used to cut rebates of various widths. Self-guiding cutters can be used for edge-profiling straight, curved or irregular-shaped workpieces, but as the pilot, pin or bearing, faithfully follows the contour of the material or template it will also pick up any irregularities (such as dents, glue spots, proud knots), which will show up as unevenness in the line of the trimmed edge, moulding or rebate. It is therefore important to remove or fill any edge defects before starting the cut.

4 Overhead and Inverted Routers

OPPOSITE ABOVE
Fig. 37 The Trend 11/30 STA overhead routing stand takes most router heads including high frequency motors powered via a static invertor from a single phase supply, and can be used for 'pin' routing for repetitive batch work.

OPPOSITE BELOW
Fig. 38 Bench-mounted overhead router stands offer many of the facilities of floor standing machines but are generally side lever operated although hydraulic foot operation is fitted to some proprietary stands (mainly USA).

For many routing applications, in particular repetitive copying, overhead routing machines are more convenient, safer, and offer a higher degree of control over the accuracy of the finished work than is generally possible with handheld or inverted-table routers. This is due both to the rigidity of the cutting head and to the visibility afforded to the cutting operation (see Figs 37 and 38).

To achieve this control the routing head is mounted on a vertical slide supported on a rigid horizontal arm. The slide is operated either by a side lever as on a pillar drill, or a foot pedal via a pneumatic or mechanical linkage. This arrangement allows the cutter to be lowered at precisely 90° into the workpiece to a preset depth of cut.

Both bench-mounted and free-standing machines are available (from Trend and other manufacturers), generally powered by single-phase portable router motors mounted on the vertical slide. For heavy-duty and continuous production work a three-phase high-frequency motor with variable speed should be fitted, powered via a static frequency invertor from a single-phase supply. (Inventor changing single phase (220/240 volts) 50 cycles mains supply to three phase (165 volts) 300 cycles.)

Although bench-mounted stands are more compact and ideal for the small workshop where floor space is at a premium, foot-operated free-standing machines are more convenient, leaving both hands free to hold and guide the workpiece. Some bench stands are fitted with a pneumatic foot control to overcome this problem, but this necessitates connection to a suitable air compressor.

The depth of stroke (the depth by which the cutter can be lowered) varies between different makes of machine, but is generally around 50mm. This is adequate for most operations and to accommodate standard cutter lengths. On Trend machines, however, a further 115mm adjustment is allowed for by a slotted motor bracket mounting to accommodate longer cutters or thicker workpieces. Perfect alignment at 90° to the table is maintained by a keyway machined in the slide face but removing the key from the back of the bracket the motor can be canted at any angle up to 45° to either side, allowing angular cuts to be made. Free-standing Trend stands also offer the facility of mounting the motor beneath the table for use as an inverted router table for light spindle work.

Safety Tip

Before machining on the overhead router ensure that the clear plastic cutter guard is fitted and in place. When using handheld routers or an inverted router table, wear safety goggles with side protection (do not rely on ordinary glasses) or a full-face visor.

Clamping the Work

To facilitate clamping to the 13mm plate steel table on Trend machines a series of threaded holes are provided through the table surface. These can be used to locate hold-down clamps or pressure clamps of the Shaw guard type (see Fig. 39). For pin routing or inverted router table use, the flat machined surface of the table is particularly suited for use with vacuum-clamped templates (see page 27). However, to ensure that the operator's fingers remain well clear of the cutter and to give maximum grip and control of the work when using templates for pin routing or edge profiling, particularly of small items, a work form carrier should be used. The carrier consists of a flat tray with side handles to the under side of which the template is secured. The workpiece or material is mounted on top of the carrier aligned with the template below.

Machining on the Overhead Router

The overhead router lends itself well to everyday straight machining operations such as edge moulding, rebating, and grooving. It is also ideal for panel edge and face profiling, its rigidity and precision allowing the use of large-diameter cutters (see page 44) as well as heavy-duty jointing cutters such as the finger and corner mitre profiles (see page 112). For all these operations the table should be fitted with a split fence preferably with adjustable cheek faces (see Fig. 39). The face ends should be closed up on the cutter, leaving just adequate clearance for waste to clear. The fence offered by Trend for use on their range of machines incorporates a dust extraction take-off for connection to a high-velocity low-volume extract unit.

When machining, the cutting head fitted with the appropriate cutter is lowered into the work and locked at the required depth of cut or profile (see Fig. 40) and the material is fed against the direction of the cutter rotation. To facilitate cutting to the full depth of cut in steps, a three-position turret stop is fitted to the Trend machines (see Fig. 41).

When handling long or wide materials, roller supports or a rigid table extension should be used to support the work on a level plane.

Drilling Operations

The overhead router is also ideal for many drilling and boring operations. However, if straight fluted cutters are used they must be raised frequently to clear the waste. Spiral cutters or router drill bits are better as they lift the waste up out of the hole. It is also far safer than handheld routers for cutting large-diameter holes over 25mm. Holes in excess of this diameter may need to be plunge cut in steps of 12mm or less, depending on the material being cut, and at a reduced speed. For example, when using hinge-sinking cutters the hole should be cut in two steps using a variable-speed router motor to restrict the cutting speed to around 10,000 rpm.

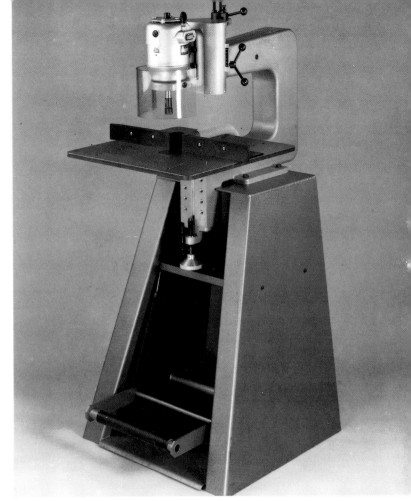

▲ FIG. 37 · ▼ FIG. 38

RIGHT Fig. 40
A stationary router head is essential when using large diameter cutters such as the fielded panel cutter. The routing head shown is a high frequency motor used for continous production work.

RIGHT Fig. 40
A stationary router head is essential when using large diameter cutters such as the fielded panel cutter. The routing head shown is a high frequency motor used for continous production work.

BELOW Fig. 39
Generally, the machine table carries an adjustable pin routing guide and is drilled and threaded to accept clamps or positioning and holding jigs.

▲ **FIG. 40** · ▼ **FIG. 39**

When drilling or boring holes in similar or repetitive workpieces, positioning blocks or a jig can be clamped or bolted to the table for fast centring (see Fig. 42).

Profiling

Edge-profiling and trimming operations using self-guiding cutters rely on a precise angle being maintained between the cutter and face of the work to ensure an even clean cut. This can best be achieved by using a fixed router, which alleviates the problem of imbalance associated with handheld routers. However, using the overhead router, as opposed to both the handheld and inverted router, also has the benefit that the under side of the material is in contact with the machine base or table, which avoids any marring on the face of the work.

All types and sizes of self-guiding cutter can be used with the overhead router but bearing-guided cutters are generally preferable to fixed-pin pilot cutters. For most applications where the full width of the edge is to be trimmed or where there is insufficient edge to engage the bearing it is

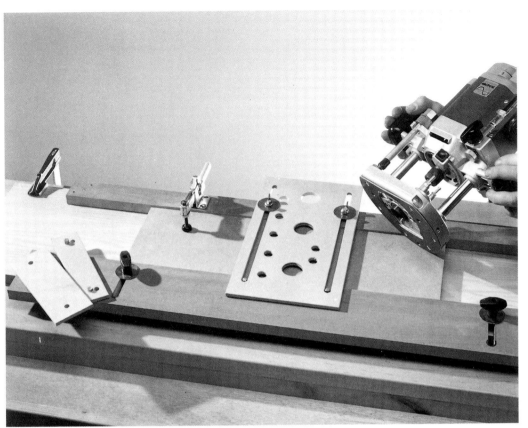

LEFT Fig. 42 A template is used on this simple drilling jig to produce repetitive or evenly spaced holes or slots while quickly and precisely aligning the work relative to the cutter.

BELOW Fig. 41 As with handheld machines, overhead stationary routers are fitted with turret depth stops to faciitate cutting in limited steps to avoid overloading the routing head.

necessary to mount the workpiece on a base or template cut to the required contour (see Fig. 43). Otherwise the bearing guide can simply follow the edge contour of the workpiece itself.

Pin Routing

The main advantage of the overhead machine is its guide-pin facility for copy and template work. This consists of a steel pin held in an eccentric flush socket set into the table. In use the pin is centred to align precisely with the cutter above and is raised to protrude above the table surface. By fixing a master template to the under side of the workpiece and locating it over the pin, the work can be moved in a controlled path beneath the lowered cutter, following and reproducing the template contour. However, to copy the shape precisely a cutter of the same diameter as the pin must be used. To accommodate cutters of different sizes, interchangeable pins can be inserted, the ends of each being turned to a different diameter to match the most common range of cutters. Pins can also be purpose-turned

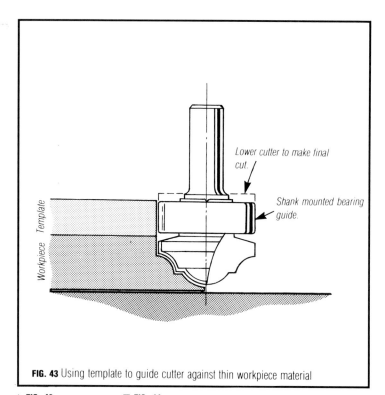

FIG. 43 Using template to guide cutter against thin workpiece material

▲ FIG. 43   ▼ FIG. 44

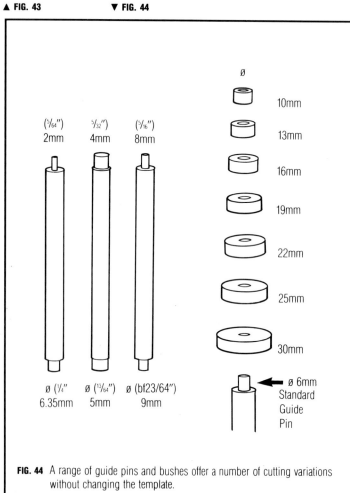

FIG. 44 A range of guide pins and bushes offer a number of cutting variations without changing the template.

to non-standard diameters to suit specific cutters. Variations on the design can be produced from the original template by using cutters of different size and profile as well as by altering the depth of cut or pin diameter. Other variations can be achieved by fitting a large-diameter guide bush over the standard 6mm pin (see Fig. 44).

Spinning

Circular cutting and profiling operations to produce gaskets and templates as well as decorative items such as plaques, frames and shallow bowls can be performed on the overhead router using a spinning technique (see Fig. 45). To 'spin' the workpiece it is rotated on a centre pin protruding from the table surface at a set radius from the cutter.

A shallow hole is drilled in the under side of either the work or a sub-base fitted beneath it, to locate over a pin or tapered point of matching diameter set into a flat table. The table is then clamped beneath the overhead router with the pin at a set distance from the cutter to give the required circle radius. The workpiece can then be located over the pin and, with the cutter lowered into the material and locked at the required depth of cut, it is rotated against the direction of rotation of the cutter (clockwise). By varying the cutting depth and type and size of cutter, different circular profiles can be achieved.

To avoid the need to reposition the table to change the circle radius an adjustable sliding centre point can be fitted to the table. This can consist of a flat dovetail edged strip with a 6mm pin fixed at one end. The strip should be set flush into the surface (use a router cutter of equal diameter to the width of the strip to cut the recess, finishing along each edge with a dovetail cutter) and be fitted with a thumbscrew or overcentre clamp to lock it in position (see Fig. 46).

Other Overhead Routing Machines

The router can also be used in the overhead position fitted into a sliding carriage for such applications as panel cutting, dado trenching and edge trimming. Several proprietary machines are available which can be adapted for use in this way.

Vertical Panel Tracking Router

Generally used with a circular saw head to cut panel products such as plywood, chipboard and other sheet materials, the panel tracking frame allows parallel cuts to be at any point along its width or length. The sheet material is held vertically in the frame with the cutting head carried on a sliding carriage running along a vertical track itself sliding along fixed tracks at either end (see Fig. 48). With the saw replaced by a router fitted with an appropriate cutter, grooves, trenchings, dovetail housings and many other cuts can be made in either direction across the face of the panel parallel to the edges.

The main benefit of this type of machine is the ease with which it can handle large sheets which are often too cumbersome and fatiguing for a single operator to handle and machine on his own.

Smaller versions of this type of machine are available for general cross-cutting and panel-trimming applications (see Fig. 49).

▲ FIG. 45 · ▼ FIG. 46

ABOVE Fig. 45 The position of the guide pin can be varied in relation to the cutter using the eccentric mount inset into the table. Further variations can be achieved using different diameter guide pins or bushes.

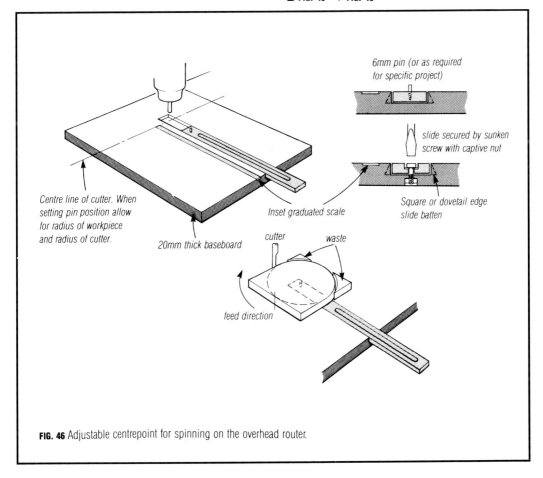

6mm pin (or as required for specific project)

slide secured by sunken screw with captive nut

Square or dovetail edge slide batten

Inset graduated scale

Centre line of cutter. When setting pin position allow for radius of workpiece and radius of cutter.

20mm thick baseboard

cutter

waste

feed direction

FIG. 46 Adjustable centrepoint for spinning on the overhead router.

▲ **FIG. 47**

ABOVE Fig. 47 The Onsrud 2003 (made in the USA but now available in the UK) features a cast frame and pin arm mounted on a welded sheet steel base unit. Both the pin and router head are retractable.

OPPOSITE ABOVE Fig. 48 Vertical panel routers ensure precise parallel cutting across the face of the material.

OPPOSITE BELOW Fig. 49 The SSC horizontal panel router is limited to widths of less than 915mm

Radial-Arm Saw

Many radial-arm saws, such as those marketed by Black & Decker under the DeWalt name, can be adapted to carry routers. This offers an attractive second use for the radial-arm saw, permitting many cross-cutting, jointing, mitre-cutting and panel-trimming applications (see Fig. 50).

Drilling and Milling Stands

For occasional use low-powered routers having detachable motors clamped to the plunge base by a 43mm-diameter collar can be mounted in a vertical drill stand. Although generally intended for use with low-speed power drills, fitted to a rigid machining table incorporating a suitable fence, cutter guarding and hold-down clamps, this arrangement can be used for many light-duty applications, including plunge drilling using the side ratchet lever (see Fig. 51).

Inverted Router

The portable router can be effectively used as a light-duty spindle moulder by mounting it inverted beneath a rigid table with the cutter protruding up through a central opening. The table should be fitted with a straight fence incorporating a rear cutter guard and have provision for sprung hold-down guards (Shaw guards) to ensure that the material is held firmly during specific machining operations. By mounting the portable router by its base or the side fence rods as on the ELU accessory tables, adjustment of the depth of cut, including the use of the turret stop or fine-depth adjuster, can be carried out as when using the router as a handheld machine. As with all routing operations the direction of feed is against the direction of rotation of the cutter (see Fig. 52).

Straight Rebating, Grooving and Edge Profiling

For all straight-edge work a two-section side fence should be used incorporating a rear cutter guard. The fence must be securely mounted when in use but allow parallel adjustment for width of cut and for positioning grooves across the face of the work. To ensure that the work is held under equal constant pressure to produce an even cut throughout its length, sprung hold-down guards should be carefully adjusted to ensure a smooth feed rate. For working difficult and resinous woods a PTFE 'dry' lubricant spray should be applied to the pressure pads, table surface and cutter to again maintain a smooth feed rate and prevent the build-up of resin and dust.

Straight edges are generally machined in one of two ways, either making a cut the full width of the edge (as when flush trimming or cutting a bullnose profile) or by machining only a portion of the width (as when

▲ FIG. 48 · ▼ FIG. 49

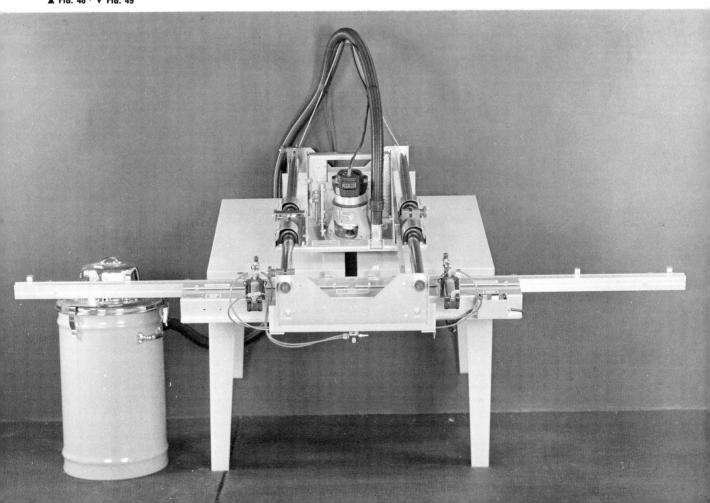

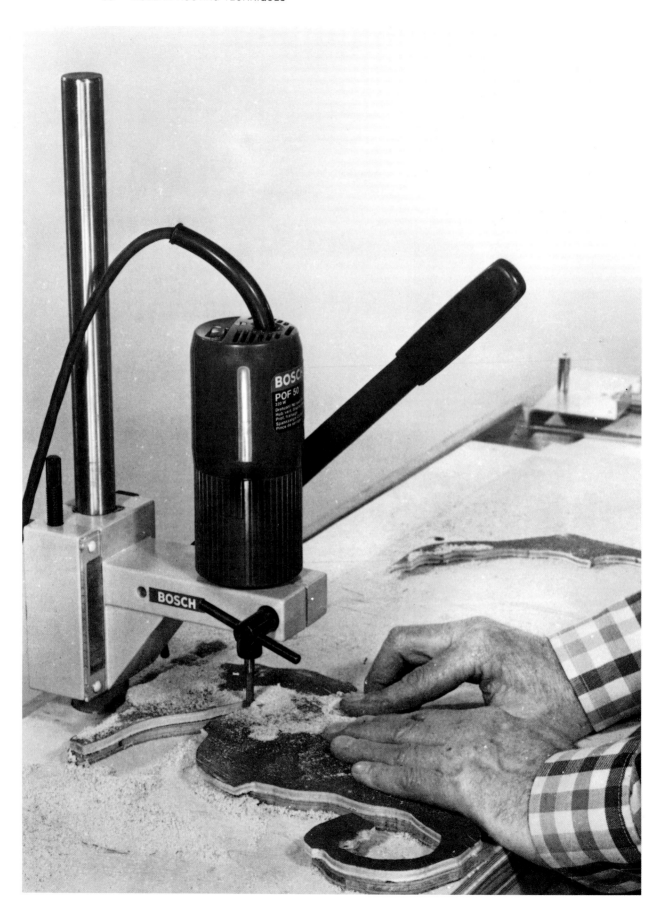

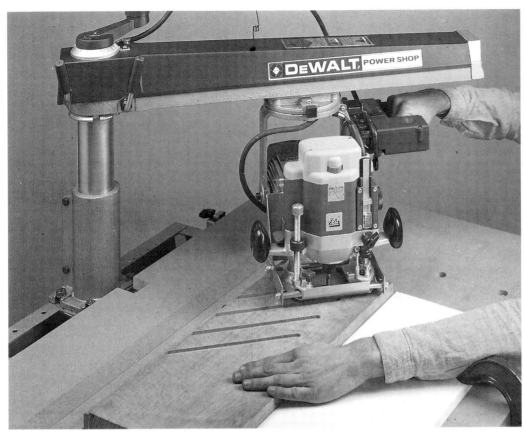

OPPOSITE Fig. 51 For light work, router motors having a 43mm collar mounting can be fitted in a vertical power drill stand. The Bosch stand is suitable for both freehand and straight cutting operations.

LEFT Fig. 50 A rigid mounting bracket fitted to the saw motor housing enables the router to be mounted on the carriage of the radial arm saw offering a versatile guide system for crosscutting, housings, mitre and bevel cuts.

LEFT Fig. 52 Tenons, halvings or rebates are easily machined on the inverted router table using a sliding mitre fence. To prevent breakout of the rear edge of the cut, a parallel batten can be held between the fence and material.

rebating or applying a moulding to the top or bottom lip only). For the latter the two faces of the side fence must be in line to support the continuous edge of the work, while for the former a stepped fence is preferable to prevent the cut edge tilting in towards the rear face of the fence and running the cut out of parallel. For those tables not fitted with separately adjustable fence faces, a purpose-made adjustable fence should be used (see Fig. 53).

When machining long lengths of materials, extension faces should be fitted to both fence faces to guide the work smoothly into and out of the cut. These should be firmly bolted or clamped to the existing fence.

As with inverted saw tables or benches, it is useful to have separate sliding square and mitre cross fences against which narrow workpieces can be held while cutting or trimming tenons, mitres or scribed ends.

Copy Routing and Edge Profiling

All types of self-guided cutters can be used for copy and edge profiling on the inverted router table following either the contour of the workpiece or a template secured above or beneath it (see Fig. 54). Alternatively, a copying arm carrying a guide bearing race

▲ **FIG. 53**   ▼ **FIG. 54**

ABOVE Fig. 53 An adjustable face on the outfeed section of the machine fence ensures that the cut edge remains parallel throughout the cutting operation.

RIGHT Fig. 54 Mitres and other angled cuts are made using the sliding mitre fence either presenting the material at an obtuse angle, or an acute angle if restricted by the table length.

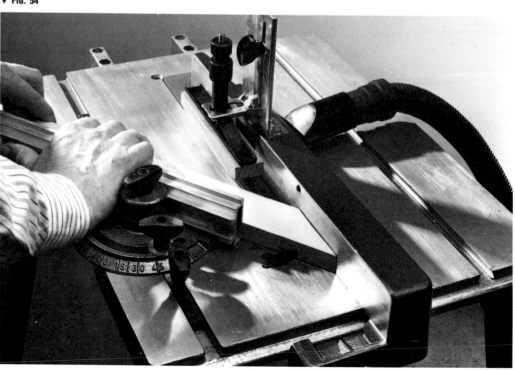

can be used centred directly over the cutter (see Fig. 55). Whenever profiling or trimming circular or irregular curved edges in this way, position an anti-kick stop finger or block before the cutter to allow the work to be fed into the cutter smoothly.

To safely rebate or mould thin battens on the inverted router table, an enclosed or tunnel guide can be clamped across the table (see Fig. 56). With the guide in position and the height of the cutter set, the bead or batten is fed in from one end against the direction of rotation of the cutter.

Large-Diameter Profile and Jointing Cutters

When using large-diameter cutters such as panel-raising cutters (see page 44) or finger-joint cutters, the router and material must be held and supported firmly. The inverted router table offers this facility, allowing accurate work to be carried out safely and efficiently. When handling large pieces or long lengths of material, however, extension supports or trestles should be positioned to support any overhang on a level plane with the table surface. When using this type and size of cutter do ensure that cutter guards are fitted and that the cutter speed is reduced to suit (see page 23).

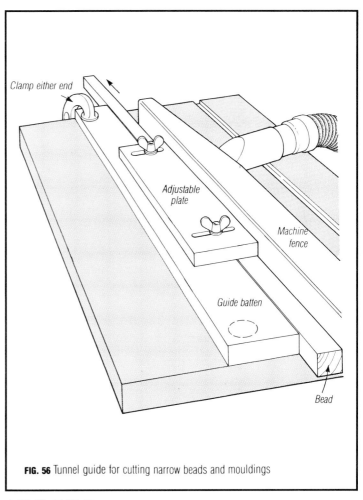

FIG. 56 Tunnel guide for cutting narrow beads and mouldings

▲ **FIG. 56** · ▼ **FIG. 55**

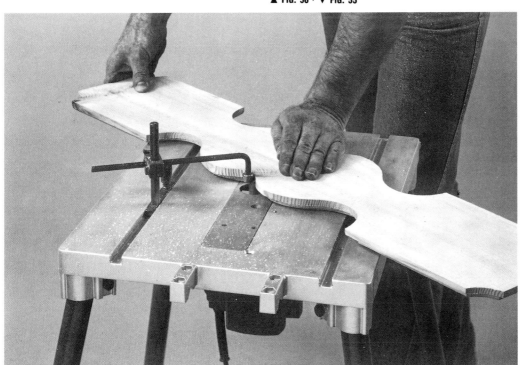

LEFT Fig. 55 When trimming or moulding shaped work, the edge or the edge of a template, can be run against a copy arm guide bearing mounted over the cutter.

Safety Tip

When edge profiling using self-guiding cutters or a copying arm, the cutter is often left exposed. To reduce the risk of personal injury a clear plastic circular guard or ring guard (as used on spindle moulders) can be easily mounted above the cutter or the guide arm.

5 | Straight Guides

For the majority of straight line trimming and cutting operations along or parallel to the edge of the workpiece, the router is guided by the adjustable side fence. For straight cuts across the face of the material, however, it is necessary to clamp a straight edge or guide across the work against which the base of the router can run.

Side Fence

For straight grooves, rebates, mouldings and edge trimming, working parallel to the edge of the material or workpiece, the side fence (as supplied with most machines) is fitted to the router base, the width of the cut being set by locking the fence to its slide rods with the threaded knobs. For making micro-adjustments some manufacturers offer as an optional extra a fine-adjustment screw which fits between the base of the router and the side fence (see Fig. 1 page 8).

When using the side fence care must be taken to keep it against the face of the workpiece or guide, not allowing it to lift away from the edge and run out of parallel, in particular as it leaves the cut. To reduce this tendency most side fences are fitted with plastic faces that can be adjusted to suit the cutter diameter and the type of material and/or operation. During coarse fast cutting, leave adequate clearance between the ends of the faces and the cutter to allow large chips to clear; when fine trimming, leave minimal clearance to minimize any tendency for the fence to turn in as the cutter reaches the end of workpiece. On some routers, such as those in the ELU range, the angle section faces can be mounted the opposite way round for trimming along narrow-profile edges or flush-trimming plastic laminates when one or both surfaces have been applied and overlap the edge (see page 100).

Where the workpiece is of insufficient length to guide the side fence smoothly in and out the cut, longer face battens cut from parallel timber or plastic strip can be fitted. These are secured through the holes that take the screws used to retain the manufacturer's plastic face linings (see Fig. 57). Where the cutter needs to be centred along the face line of the fence or set back into it, a pair of longer linings can be used, leaving a gap between the meeting ends to accommodate the cutter diameter as before.

For certain operations, such as when forming multiple-cut mouldings (see page 169), the side fence can be run against the opposite edge to the one being cut, but do ensure that both edges are parallel to start with as any variations in the width of the cut may slow or start to jam the cutter, pulling it off parallel and further into the wood. Also ensure that the guiding edge of the workpiece is straight and smooth to avoid similar problems.

Whenever possible use overcut boards at both ends of the workpiece to prevent breakout, maintain level support for the router, and guide the side fence as the cutter enters and leaves the cut (see Fig. 12 page 22).

For accurate alignment when mortising or grooving along the narrow edge of a rail or panel, a second fence can be fitted on the slide rods but on the opposite side of the router base (see Fig. 58). Set both side fences to position or centre the mortise, using the fine adjusting screw to make the final adjustments, but leaving a minimal clearance to prevent binding. To precisely centre a mortise or groove across the width of the workpiece, centre the cutter as accurately as possible, then make the cut, and finish by reversing the router so that each fence runs against the opposite face and make the final passes in the opposite direction.

When cutting rebates or mouldings round the inside edges of frames, as when increasing glazing rebates to take double glazed sealed units, a secondary square base cut from MDF (medium density fibreboard) can be screwed beneath the side fence diagonally lined with the cutter. This allows the router to be guided right into the corners, the angled fence stopping against the faces of both frame members (see Fig. 59). Set the cutter proud of the corner of the square, measuring the required width of the rebate or moulding equally from both faces. A cutter equal to the width of the required cut is recommended for this type of operation, the depth of cut being set in the usual way and increased for each pass until the final depth is reached, finishing with a fine skimming cut to remove any burn or cutter marks.

Straight Edges and Frames

Other methods of guiding the router in a straight line involve running it against a straight edge or between parallel straight edges forming a frame, in either case held firmly across the workpiece to prevent any movement during the cutting operation.

The simplest form of straight guide can be a batten or strip of sheet material cut to suit the width or length of the workpiece, held by clamps, double-sided tape, or pins or by some other convenient method that is both secure and will not hinder the smooth continuous feed of the router. The edge of the guide must obviously be true, especially when used for edge trimming. Strips at least 100mm wide cut from the edge of stable sheet materials such as MDF (medium density fibreboard) are more suitable than natural timber and the pre-cut edges are

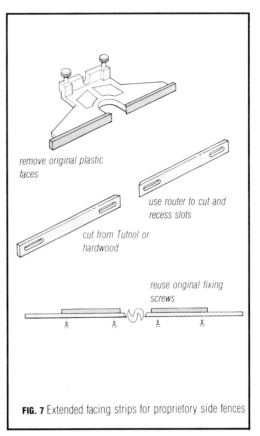

remove original plastic faces

use router to cut and recess slots

cut from Tufnol or hardwood

reuse original fixing screws

FIG. 7 Extended facing strips for proprietory side fences

BELOW Fig. 58 To ensure that mortises, grooves or mouldings are perfectly centred across the edge of the workpiece, twin side fences can be fitted, one either side of the base.

▲ **FIG. 57** · ▼ **FIG. 58**

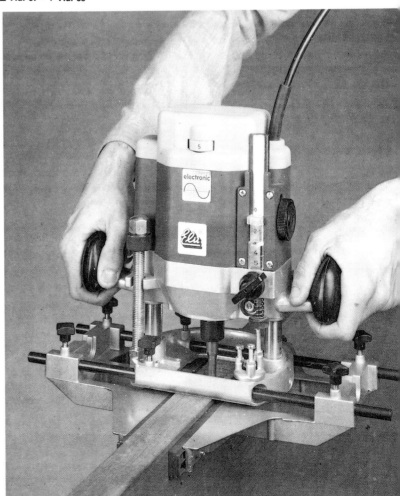

▲ **FIG. 59**

ABOVE Fig. 59 A simple homemade right angled fence fitted diagonally to the side fence rods is particularly useful when increasing the rebate depth of existing glazed frames to take replacement double glazing units.

⚠ ☐ Safety Tip

Ensure that the router is firmly held and well balanced. Adopt a balanced stance that allows you to follow through to complete the cut without overreaching or losing your balance. Ensure that the work is securely held by clamps or a jig to leave both hands free to control and operate the router.

---

generally square and true without further trimming.

Although thin hardboard can be used for light work, straight guides should be at least 6mm thick to ensure that the router base does not ride up over them. Whenever the work allows, always make the guides of an adequate length to overhang the workpiece by the length of the router base at each end in order to support and keep the router in line as it enters and leaves the cut.

When positioning the straight edge the distance between the cutter and the edge of the router base must be allowed for. Either set out this distance on the face of the work, measuring from the line of the cut to the face of the straight edge, or alternatively use the router fitted with the appropriate cutter to set the distance. If using the latter, do check that the cutter is withdrawn fractionally below the face of the router base to prevent the tip scratching the surface of the workpiece either side of the cut line. To save time when setting out, it is well worth cutting a series of spacer gauges or a notched gauge (see Fig. 60) to suit the diameter of the cutter, positioning them between the line of the cut and the straight edge on the surface of the workpiece. Although it is often suggested that a hinged gauge can be fitted to the straight edge, which can be folded back once the distance is set, this type of addition tends to over-complicate the guide, increases the overall thickness of the template, and generally gets in the way. A more precise method is to make up a stepped guide to suit specific cutters by gluing thin sheet (3–6mm) beneath the guide over which the router can slide once the distance has been set. Although this reduces the depth of cut possible by the thickness of the material, it is particularly useful when routing polished or easily marred surfaces, and will support the router over uneven or broken surfaces such as when cutting across an open grille or spaced rails.

A stepped guide is of particular use for trimming square edges and mitres, the edge of the gauge being set against the cut line and the cut made with an appropriate cutter (see Fig. 61). To make up a stepped guide accurately, glue the gauge sheet, cut slightly

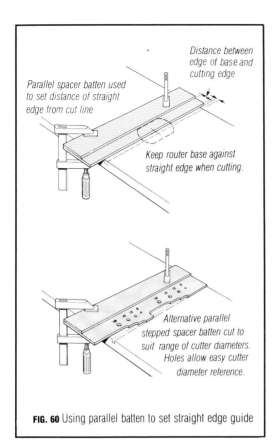

Parallel spacer batten used to set distance of straight edge from cut line

Distance between edge of base and cutting edge

Keep router base against straight edge when cutting.

Alternative parallel stepped spacer batten cut to suit range of cutter diameters. Holes allow easy cutter diameter reference.

FIG. 60 Using parallel batten to set straight edge guide

▲ **FIG. 60**

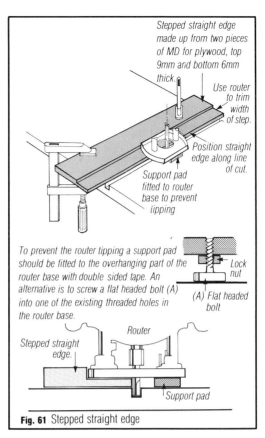

Stepped straight edge made up from two pieces of MD for plywood, top 9mm and bottom 6mm thick.

Use router to trim width of step.

Position straight edge along line of cut.

Support pad fitted to router base to prevent tipping

To prevent the router tipping a support pad should be fitted to the overhanging part of the router base with double sided tape. An alternative is to screw a flat headed bolt (A) into one of the existing threaded holes in the router base.

Lock nut

(A) Flat headed bolt

Router

Stepped straight edge.

Support pad

Fig. 61 Stepped straight edge

▲ **FIG. 61** · ▼ **FIG. 62**

BELOW Fig. 62 The ELU tracking attachment is used for crosscuts or housing across narrow boards, the blade sliding in the channel clamped to the workpiece, and can be fitted to most routers having 8 or 10mm diameter side fence rods.

over width, to the underside of the straight edge and trim to the precise width by running the router fitted with the appropriate cutter against the straight edge. Leave adequate length either end to allow the cutter to follow through and clear the cut, or fit stops to limit the length of travel when cutting spaced slots and stub tenons.

A proprietary straight guide or tracking fence is available from ELU accessory range for use with all ELU routers. It consists of a grooved nylon track which clamps to the workpiece and an aluminium tracking fence which is attached to one of the router's standard side fence bars (see Fig. 62). In use the tracking fence slides in the groove, keeping the router on a precise line. PTFE dry lubricant can be sprayed on the track to ensure that the fence slides with a smooth continuous movement.

A straight edge guide can be used at any angle across the workpiece, always spaced from the cut line as before. To speed up the setting out, a stock (as on a T-square) can be fixed to one end of the straight edge either at 90° or at another predetermined angle,

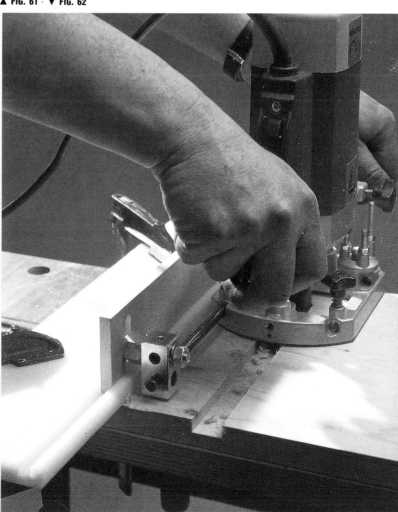

▲ FIG. 63

ABOVE Fig. 63 One of the simplest ways of guiding the router is against a straight edge or T-square clamped across the face of the board with g-clamps or a sliding stock. Overcut battens should always be used to prevent breakout.

▼ FIG. 64

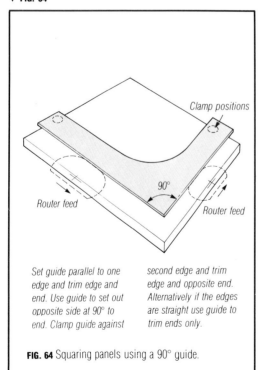

Clamp positions

90°

Router feed

Router feed

Set guide parallel to one edge and trim edge and end. Use guide to set out opposite side at 90° to end. Clamp guide against

second edge and trim edge and opposite end. Alternatively if the edges are straight use guide to trim ends only.

FIG. 64 Squaring panels using a 90° guide.

▼ FIG. 65

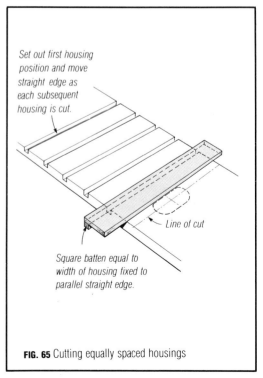

Set out first housing position and move straight edge as each subsequent housing is cut.

Line of cut

Square batten equal to width of housing fixed to parallel straight edge.

FIG. 65 Cutting equally spaced housings

while a second sliding stock can be fitted to both position and secure the guide across the workpiece (see Fig. 63). To trim two edges or to cut a groove, slot or moulding along two sides to form a precise angle, a double-edged guide can be used (see Fig. 64).

If a lip or batten is fitted to the edge or under side of a straight edge parallel to the guide face, it can be used to accurately space grooves, slots or housings in the construction of shelf units or other items with evenly spaced divisions. Guiding the router in this fashion not only ensures precise parallel spacing but once the first groove or slot is cut there is no need to set out the remainder (see Fig. 65). An alternative but similar method to this is to use a parallel-edged board cut to the width between the grooves minus the width of the router base and a separate batten. The first groove is cut against one edge of the board and the batten, cut slightly thicker than the depth of cut, is

pressed into it. The board is butted up to the batten and the second groove cut against the opposite edge. By fitting the stop batten in each consecutive groove a series of equally spaced housings can be cut quickly and accurately with either straight or dove-tail cutters.

Parallel Straight Edges

If the router is run between two parallel joined straight edges, any risk of it pulling away from the guide face is eliminated. Furthermore, by setting the guides wider than the router base or at an angle, wide or tapered housings and slots can be cut by first working against one straight edge and then back against the other, finally removing the waste from between the two cuts (see Fig. 66). Stopped housings or slots can be cut by fitting stops at the appropriate positions along one or both straight edges. When making up parallel (or tapered) guides with a stock at each end to hold the battens paral-

ABOVE Fig. 66   Twin parallel straight edges set apart by the width of the router base prevent the router from running off course. Alternatively, they can be set further apart for cutting wide housings, recesses or apertures.

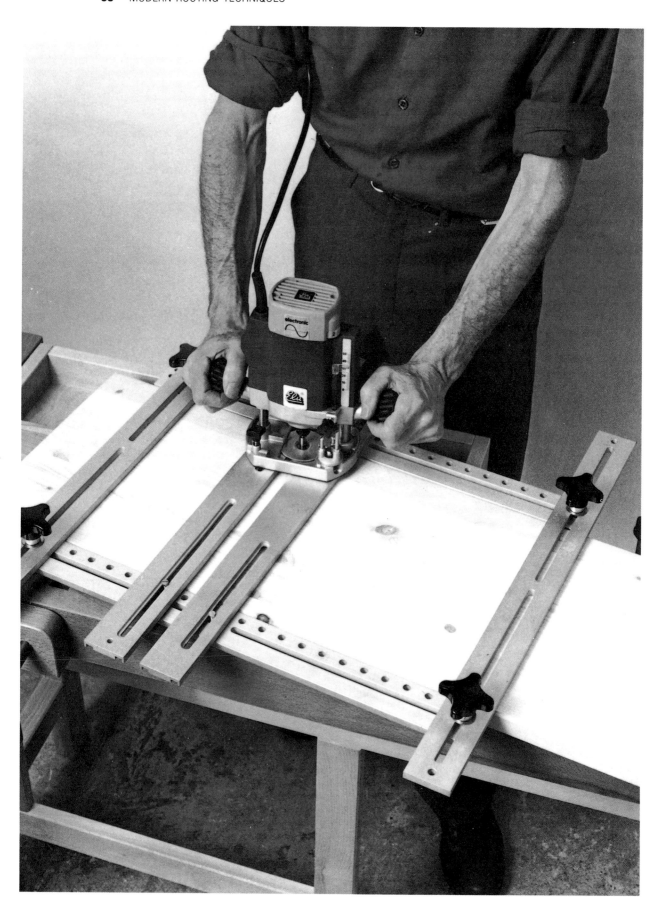

lel (or at the required angle), use material of adequate thickness for the stocks to accommodate the cutter depth as it will cut across these as it enters and leaves the cut.

Proprietary universal parallel guides are also available, such as the Varijig from Trend which is adjustable for both straight or angled cutting across as well as for many other routing operations (see Figs 67, 68 and 69). The guide consists of flat slotted aluminium sections connected by clamping knobs. The frame is assembled loose over the workpiece with waste battens along either edge to allow for overcut. Two pairs of guide rails are supplied, one pair to clamp the frame together and guide the router, the rails being set in position using a square or bevel gauge before being tightened. Adjustable pegs located in a series of equally spaced holes (25mm centres or, with the bars reversed, 12·5mm centres) along the second pair of guide rails allow quick precise spacing when cutting a series of housings or slots.

◀ **FIG. 67** · ▼ **FIG. 69**   ▲ **FIG. 68**

OPPOSITE Fig. 67 The variable frame guide jig offers an accurate and fast method of setting out and guiding the router and can be used as a straight guide for housings, or an internal guide frame for cutting recesses and apertures.

LEFT Fig. 69 The side rails of the Varijig are also drilled to take loose pins for positioning the guide bars when making evenly spaced parallel crosscuts. Shown is an open timber grille cut using this method.

ABOVE Fig. 68 The Varijig from Trend consists of a frame made up from slotted aluminium sections with clamps across the workpiece and carries the router guide rails.

6 Templates and Guide Bushes

Templates lend themselves to a wide and comprehensive range of router application. They are particularly suited, but not limited, to repetitive batch production operations. Setting up the router for template work, whether handheld, overhead or inverted is fairly simple, requiring little time and minimal cost. However, as with all pattern making, time and care are needed in the design and production of the template itself to ensure accurate clean cutting of the finished workpiece.

To guide the handheld router against the edge of the template a guide bush or a bearing guided cutter is fitted to the router (for overhead and inverted template routing see pages 42 and 48).

Guide Bushes

Guide bushes are available in a range of diameters not only to accommodate cutters of various sizes but to facilitate in cutting stepped work from a single template (see Fig. 70). Most guide bushes take the form of a flanged ring fitted to the under side of the router base by two mounting screws, although ELU have now reintroduced their retractable guide bush system on some of their range, allowing adjustment for template materials of various thicknesses as well as speeding up the setting-up time (see Fig. 1 page 8). Most manufacturers use the former type and tend to follow a standard flange diameter and fixing hole centres, allowing a more comprehensive range of bushes such as those available from Trend to be used with their machines. Machines which do not accept this standard can

generally be adapted by fitting a sub-base (generally available from the guide bush supplier) which is machined to take the standard guide bush flange and is supplied with a centring pin to ensure precise alignment in relation to the collet and cutter.

When selecting guide bushes ensure that there is adequate clearance between the inside face of the bush and the cutter, not only to avoid damage to the cutter and bush but to ensure that chips and waste can clear freely. When cutting deep cavities choose a guide bush of the largest diameter possible to allow waste to clear freely and prevent it packing round the cutter, which can lead to overheating and burning. Most common makes of guide bush are about 6·5mm deep with a wall thickness of 1·5mm. If the template material is less than this the bush can be ground or filed down slightly. To maintain a level end on the bush, drill a hole the diameter of the bush in a piece of material fractionally thinner than that of the template, press the guide bush through the hole and clamp it under the material. File the bush flush with the surface and finish by carefully deburring both the inner and outer edges.

When fitting flange-type bushes do check that the fixing screw heads lie below the face of the router base plate when tightened to avoid damaging the surface of the workpiece.

Bearing-Guided Cutters

Bearing-guided cutters with a guide bearing mounted at the end or above the cutter on its shank can also be used to follow a template. Interchangeable bearings of diffe-

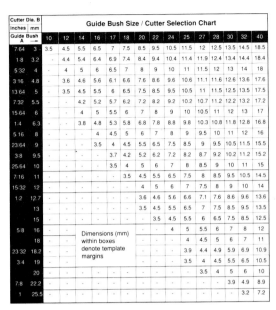

Guide Bush Size / Cutter Selection Chart

Cutter Dia. B (inches)	mm	10	12	14	16	17	18	20	22	24	26	27	28	30	32	40
7/64	3	3.5	4.5	5.5	6.5	7	7.5	8.5	9.5	10.5	11.5	12	12.5	13.5	14.5	18.5
1/8	3.2	-	4.4	5.4	6.4	6.9	7.4	8.4	9.4	10.4	11.4	11.9	12.4	13.4	14.4	18.4
5/32	4	-	4	5	6	6.5	7	8	9	10	11	11.5	12	13	14	18
3/16	4.8	-	3.6	4.6	5.6	6.1	6.6	7.6	8.6	9.6	10.6	11.1	11.6	12.6	13.6	17.6
13/64	5	-	3.5	4.5	5.5	6	6.5	7.5	8.5	9.5	10.5	11	11.5	12.5	13.5	17.5
7/32	5.5	-	-	4.2	5.2	5.7	6.2	7.2	8.2	9.2	10.2	10.7	11.2	12.2	13.2	17.2
15/64	6	-	-	4	5	5.5	6	7	8	9	10	10.5	11	12	13	17
1/4	6.3	-	-	3.8	4.8	5.3	5.8	6.8	7.8	8.8	9.8	10.3	10.8	11.8	12.8	16.8
5/16	8	-	-	-	4	4.5	5	6	7	8	9	9.5	10	11	12	16
23/64	9	-	-	-	3.5	4	4.5	5.5	6.5	7.5	8.5	9	9.5	10.5	11.5	15.5
3/8	9.5	-	-	-	-	3.7	4.2	5.2	6.2	7.2	8.2	8.7	9.2	10.2	11.2	15.2
25/64	10	-	-	-	-	3.5	4	5	6	7	8	8.5	9	10	11	15
7/16	11	-	-	-	-	-	3.5	4.5	5.5	6.5	7.5	8	8.5	9.5	10.5	14.5
15/32	12	-	-	-	-	-	-	4	5	6	7	7.5	8	9	10	14
1/2	12.7	-	-	-	-	-	-	3.6	4.6	5.6	6.6	7.1	7.6	8.6	9.6	13.6
	13	-	-	-	-	-	-	3.5	4.5	5.5	6.5	7	7.5	8.5	9.5	13.5
	15	-	-	-	-	-	-	-	3.5	4.5	5.5	6	6.5	7.5	8.5	12.5
5/8	16	-	-	-	-	-	-	-	-	4	5	5.5	6	7	8	12
	18	-	-	-	-	-	-	-	-	-	4	4.5	5	6	7	11
23/32	18.2	-	-	-	-	-	-	-	-	-	3.9	4.4	4.9	5.9	6.9	10.9
3/4	19	-	-	-	-	-	-	-	-	-	3.5	4	4.5	5.5	6.5	10.5
	20	-	-	-	-	-	-	-	-	-	-	3.5	4	5	6	10
7/8	22.2	-	-	-	-	-	-	-	-	-	-	-	-	3.9	4.9	8.9
1	25.5	-	-	-	-	-	-	-	-	-	-	-	-	-	3.2	7.2

Dimensions (mm) within boxes denote template margins

FIG. 70 Calculating Guide bush diameters and template margins.

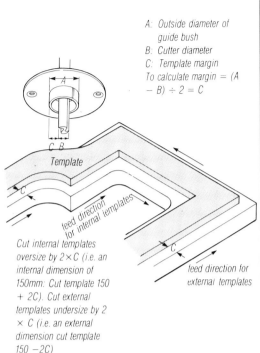

A: Outside diameter of guide bush
B: Cutter diameter
C: Template margin
To calculate margin = (A − B) ÷ 2 = C

Template

feed direction for internal templates

feed direction for external templates

Cut internal templates oversize by 2×C (i.e. an internal dimension of 150mm: Cut template 150 + 2C). Cut external templates undersize by 2 × C (i.e. an external dimension cut template 150 −2C)

BELOW Fig. 71 Many routers use a standard guide bush fitting, the bush flange being inset flush into the base held by countersunk screws. An alternative method (mainly USA) uses a threaded spigot held by an internally threaded ring.

▲ FIG. 70

▼ FIG. 71

rent outer diameters can be fitted to each type of cutter to alter the cutter distance from the template edge, effectively changing the cutter profile (see Fig. 72).

Making Templates

As the guide bush or bearing will follow its contours precisely, any template must be cut cleanly and precisely, as any faults or irregularities will be reproduced and possibly spoil the finished work. To allow for the distance between the outer face of the guide bush and the cutting edge of the cutter, templates must be cut either oversize for use when working from the internal edge or undersize when following an external edge. This oversize or undersize margin to allow for the difference between cutter and guide bush diameters can be worked out by deducting the cutter diameter from the outside guide bush diameter and dividing by two (see Fig. 70).

When making templates for insetting fittings or components choose a cutter matching or of slightly larger radius than the

corners or curves of the item in order to leave the minimum cleaning out with a gouge or, for square corners, a chisel.

When setting out a template leave an adequate area round or to the side of the cutout to provide adequate support on which to balance the router to prevent it from tipping. To prevent the router tipping when restricted to a small template area or width, arrange pads or blocks round the

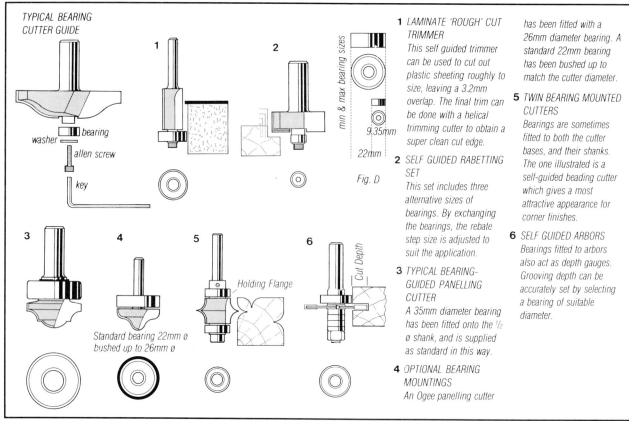

TYPICAL BEARING
CUTTER GUIDE

bearing
washer
allen screw
key

min & max bearing sizes

9.35mm

22mm

Fig. D

Standard bearing 22mm ø
bushed up to 26mm ø

Holding Flange

Cut Depth

1 *LAMINATE 'ROUGH' CUT TRIMMER*
This self guided trimmer can be used to cut out plastic sheeting roughly to size, leaving a 3.2mm overlap. The final trim can be done with a helical trimming cutter to obtain a super clean cut edge.

2 *SELF GUIDED RABETTING SET*
This set includes three alternative sizes of bearings. By exchanging the bearings, the rebate step size is adjusted to suit the application.

3 *TYPICAL BEARING-GUIDED PANELLING CUTTER*
A 35mm diameter bearing has been fitted onto the ½ ø shank, and is supplied as standard in this way.

4 *OPTIONAL BEARING MOUNTINGS*
An Ogee panelling cutter has been fitted with a 26mm diameter bearing. A standard 22mm bearing has been bushed up to match the cutter diameter.

5 *TWIN BEARING MOUNTED CUTTERS*
Bearings are sometimes fitted to both the cutter bases, and their shanks. The one illustrated is a self-guided beading cutter which gives a most attractive appearance for corner finishes.

6 *SELF GUIDED ARBORS*
Bearings fitted to arbors also act as depth gauges. Grooving depth can be accurately set by selecting a bearing of suitable diameter.

▲ **FIG. 72**   ▼ **FIG. 73**

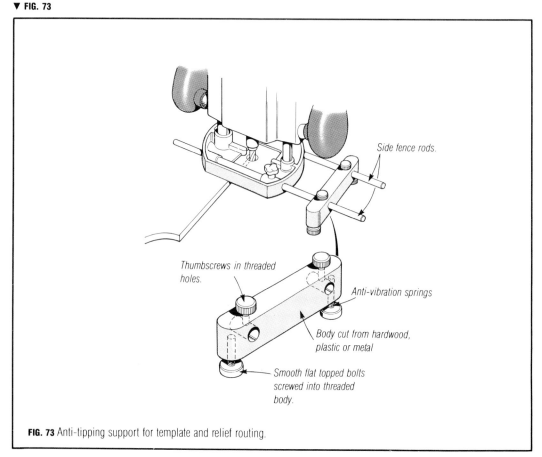

Side fence rods.

Thumbscrews in threaded holes.

Anti-vibration springs

Body cut from hardwood, plastic or metal

Smooth flat topped bolts screwed into threaded body.

FIG. 73 Anti-tipping support for template and relief routing.

workpiece the same height as the face of the template. Alternatively, the router can be supported above the template face by feet of equal height fitted to the side fence rods to sit and slide on a smooth level work surface surrounding the workpiece (see Fig. 73).

For complex patterns or multiple operations it is often worth cutting several templates, each to cut a different part of the pattern or operation. This allows each template to be simplified and avoids cutting away too much material, which would lead to a risk of distortion.

Template Material

In practice most templates tend to be made of whatever scraps are available in the workshop. However, to achieve the best results the materials used should have the following properties: they should be rigid enough to support their own weight plus that of the router over short spans; stable so that they don't distort or warp; dense enough to cut cleanly but be easily worked to a good finish; and the surface should be as flat and smooth as possible to allow the router to slide freely. Recommended

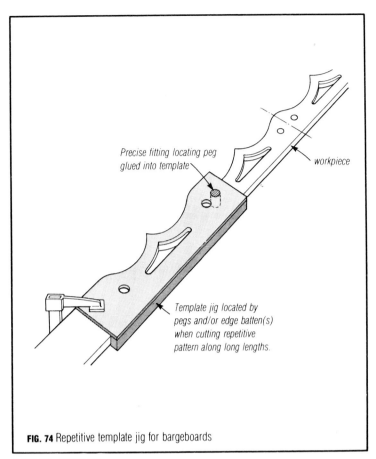

FIG. 74 Repetitive template jig for bargeboards

▲ **FIG. 74** · ▼ **FIG. 75**

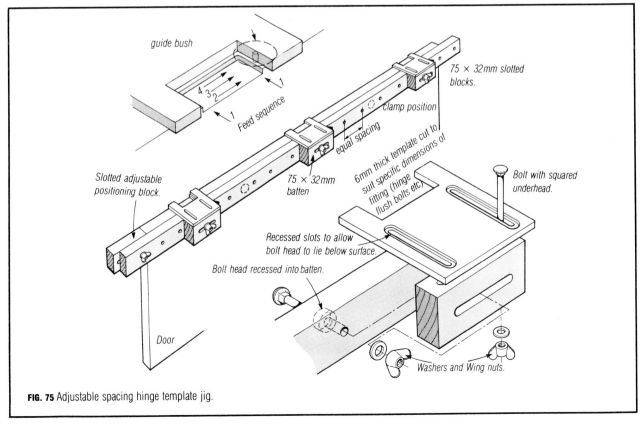

FIG. 75 Adjustable spacing hinge template jig.

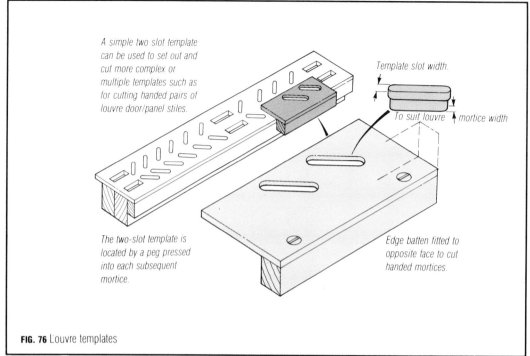

A simple two slot template can be used to set out and cut more complex or multiple templates such as for cutting handed pairs of louvre door/panel stiles.

Template slot width.

To suit louvre mortice width

The two-slot template is located by a peg pressed into each subsequent mortice.

Edge batten fitted to opposite face to cut handed mortices.

FIG. 76 Louvre templates

BELOW Fig. 77 When cutting louvre housing templates it is generally easiest to cut a pair of handed two-slot templates, using them to either cut the stiles directly, or to cut a multiple slot template for batch production.

▲ FIG. 76 · ▼ FIG. 77

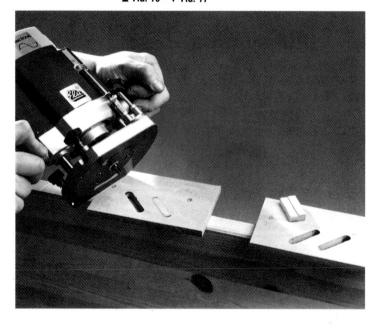

materials are: acrylic materials such as Perspex and Plexiglas, though these are rather brittle and inclined to crack; hard resinous plastics such as Tufnol, which is undoubtedly one of the best, having good machining characteristics; plastic laminates (Formica, Warerite, etc.) bonded to a thicker base material (MDF, plywood); and wood-based materials such as medium-density fibreboard (MDF) or plywood laminated from fine-grained timbers, such as birch-faced ply (Check that the core veneers have similar working properties). Blockboard- and chipboard-based materials are not really suitable because of their uneven core structure, while hardboard should be of the denser highgrade qualities, at least 6mm thick.

Ideally, the thickness of any template should be between 6mm, the minimum to guide the bush safely, and 10mm, above which the usable length of the cutter becomes unnecessarily restricted. Before starting to cut a template check the projection of the bush, the thickness of the template and the projection of the cutter to ensure that the required cutting depth can be achieved.

The sides of all templates should be cut square since any angling towards the top or bottom edges may cause the edge to give or crush under side pressure from the router or may cause the guide bush to rise up over the edge.

For quick, accurate positioning on the workpiece, centre lines can be drawn on both the template and the workpiece or the outer edges of both can be matched for alignment. Alternatively, positioning blocks or strips can be fitted or the template can be incorporated as part of a jig (see Fig. 74). When carrying out several cutting operations on the same surface (as when cutting hinge, lock and security bolt holes and

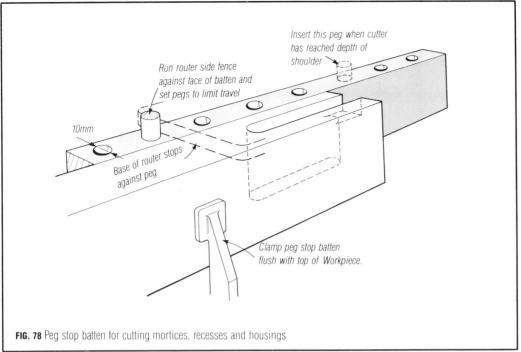

Insert this peg when cutter
has reached depth of
shoulder

Run router side fence
against face of batten and
set pegs to limit travel

10mm

Base of router stops
against peg

Clamp peg stop batten
flush with top of Workpiece.

FIG. 78 Peg stop batten for cutting mortices, recesses and housings.

▲ **FIG. 78** · ▼ **FIG. 79**

recesses along the edge of a door or the rail mortises along the inside edge of a stile) the templates can be combined into one or joined by a batten to ensure precise repetitive spacing on the jamb or matching stiles (see Fig. 75). If the template cutouts need to be evenly or equally spaced, it may be worth cutting a single template from which to set out and cut the multiple template, as in the case of the louvre template shown (Figs 76 and 77).

When fitting positioning or stiffening blocks to a template, check that they will not interfere with the smooth continuous feed of the router, that there are no metal fixings close to the edge in case the cutter runs off course, and that screws and pins are sunk below the surface to avoid interfering with or gouging into the base of the router.

Routing with Templates

Template routing offers a quick and accurate method of cutting recesses and rebates for furniture fittings and door furniture such as hinges, lock plates, flush-folding handles and name and presentation inscription plates as well as for cutting mortises, housings and decorative work.

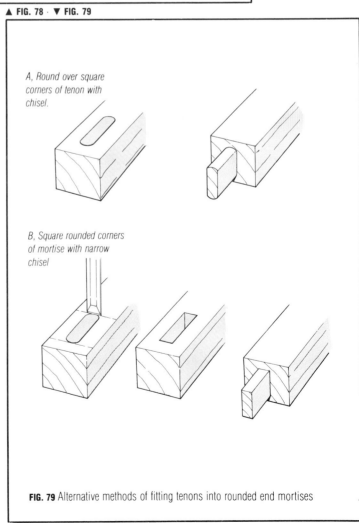

A, Round over square
corners of tenon with
chisel.

B, Square rounded corners
of mortise with narrow
chisel

FIG. 79 Alternative methods of fitting tenons into rounded end mortises

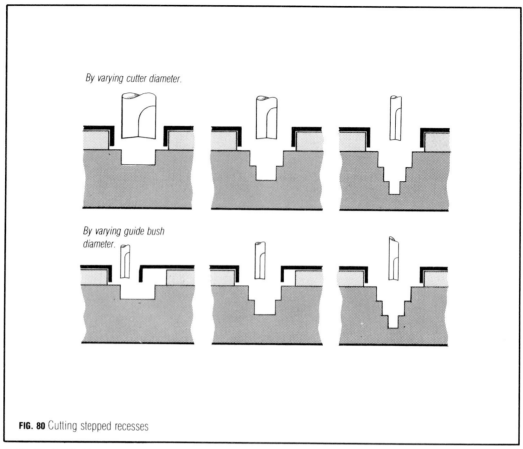

By varying cutter diameter.

By varying guide bush diameter.

FIG. 80 Cutting stepped recesses

▲ **FIG. 80** · ▼ **FIG. 81**

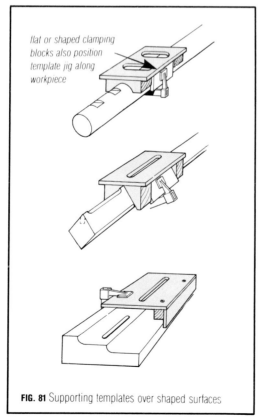

flat or shaped clamping blocks also position template jig along workpiece

FIG. 81 Supporting templates over shaped surfaces

Hinge Templates

Templates for insetting butts, back-flap and other rectangular hinges are generally cut as a simple side-entry recess, the template cut slightly oversize to allow for the difference in diameter between the cutter and guide bush and with a lip to set the position across the width of the door edge or jamb. By tapering the thickness of the template the hinge recess can be angled to give clearance between the hinged faces when closed (see Fig. 75).

Mortise Templates

The plunge action of the router can be used to great effect in cutting clean straight-sided mortises. Use a two-flute cutter or, for deep mortises, a staggered-tooth cutter, preferably of the same diameter as the width of the mortise. Always cut in several passes to allow the swarf to clear efficiently and prevent overloading the router motor. If a square shoulder recess is required a stop can be introduced once the shoulder depth is reached to reduce the length of router travel (see Fig. 78). Once the mortise is cut the round corners left by the cutter can be squared with a chisel or the corners of the tenon can be rounded to match (see Fig. 79).

Stepped Recesses

To accommodate fittings requiring a stepped recess it is necessary to cut the recess in two or more stages. If the outline of each step is the same, the original template can be often reused, with a change of either the cutter size or profile and/or the guide bush diameter. Where the outline differs a second template is used, carefully positioned over the first recess. Always cut the deepest steps first removing the waste in 3mm stages as before (see Fig. 80). Again, radiused corners left by the cutter can to be squared with chisel.

Panel Mouldings

Drawer front, door and other panels cut as one piece from sheet materials or assembled by edge-jointing narrow boards can have decorative mouldings cut into the face using either a guide bush or bearing-guided cutter to follow the template contour. When initially setting out a panel face moulding it is easiest to draw the shape on tracing film laid over the panel to see if the size, shape and positioning are in proportion before either transferring it or sticking it onto the template material and adding a margin to allow for the difference between the guide bush and cutter diameters. Cut round the contour in a smooth continuous line, finishing the edges square. Hold the template to the face or under side of the workpiece with double-sided tape or other means (see page 26) and ensure that both are firmly held to the work surface.

With the appropriate guide bush and panel face moulding cutter (see page 33) or bearing-guided cutter (see page 33) fitted in the router, check the depth of cut on scrap timber before cutting the moulding in several passes, keeping the guide bush or bearing tight against the template edge. Surface burn marks often occur at corners due to the slight hesitation as the router changes direction. These can be taken out by making a final fine skim about 1mm deep.

▲ FIG. 82 · ▼ FIG. 83

Curved or Angled Surfaces

Templates can be used for cutting openings in both concave and convex surfaces such as pipes and ductwork, or in other shapes or profiles by mounting the template at a tangent or level to the workface. This can be done by either shaping the under side of the template to match the surface profile or supporting the template on blocks to hold it above the workpiece (see Fig. 81).

Safety Tip

When machining on the overhead router or inverted table router use a push stick or pad when working close to the cutter. Always ensure that guards and eye shields are fitted and properly adjusted and that sprung hold-down (Shaw) guards are correctly tensioned to allow a smooth continuous feed.

Stair Housing Jig

Both open- and close-tread staircases can be constructed using a template to position and cut the housings in the strings to take the treads and risers. However, although a template can be cut from thin sheet material, because it is reused to make a series of cuts (that is, for each pair of treads and risers) the accumulative effect of any minor inaccuracy can easily result in an inaccurate and ill-fitting staircase. A proprietary jig such as the Trend staircase jig is not expensive in relation to the construction time saved and will ensure the precision needed for quick trouble-free on-site installation. The Trend jig can be used to construct staircases of any pitch and any rise and going, and consists of the basic template (for closed tread, an open-tread template is available separately), clamping and positioning jig and guides. Dovetail (95°) cutters are generally used for cutting the housings, the angled sides ensuring an adequate glue line and gripping into the timber faces as the wedges are driven in. A heavy-duty router is recommended, fitted with a 9·5mm or 12 mm shank cutter, with a cutting diameter to suit the thickness of the timber used for the treads and risers (see Fig. 82 and 83).

7 | Jigs

If a jig is used to position the workpiece and hold it securely, repetitive operations can be carried out with greater accuracy and much of the setting up time is eliminated. Jigs are of particular use when performing the same operation on identical or similar components or when repeating an operation involving precise spacing on a single component.

Making Jigs

As with templates, the accuracy with which the jig is constructed will be reflected in the finished work. It is therefore well worth taking time and care in the design and construction of a jig, bearing in mind the economics of the job and its possibilities for use on future projects. Again, the best materials for making jigs are those that are stable or reasonably stable, such as Tufnol, MDF, and dense fine-grain plywood, which are easily worked to a fine finish. Where jigs incorporate slides, pegs, indexing pins or catches, these should be of dense-grained hardwoods, soft metals such as aluminium or brass (in case the cutter deviates into them), or hard plastics such as Tufnol and Perspex.

The method of guiding the router can often be part of the jig, a parallel track or guide bush slot which prevents the router wandering off course being preferable to running the side fence or base of the router against the case or a single edge guide. One of the simplest methods of guiding the router is by incorporating fixed or interchangeable templates in the jig, which offers the possibility of performing highly complex

operations, or a variety of operations with the same jig.

Box Jigs

Box jigs can be used in a wide range of operations, from cutting tenon and halving joints to pre-assembly cutting of mortises and apertures for door and furniture fittings, as well as having many decorative applications in the production of mouldings and fluting on rails, legs, and beads. The box jig is generally in the form of a channel into which the workpiece is laid, the template being located in position over it by dowels or slides or as a hinged flap. Stops and shim battens can be fitted to align the workpiece with the template while length battens and stops can be used to position the cut along its length (see Fig. 84). When cutting apertures such as mortises on adjacent faces of the workpiece, an angled template can be used to allow both to be cut without repositioning the jig.

Cross-Hatch Jig

Cutters of different sizes and profiles enable various hatched and cross-hatched relief patterns, formed of equally spaced parallel lines, to be created with this jig. The workpiece is fed between overcut battens held between parallel guides, the router travelling diagonally across the workpiece guided against fixed guides set at equal opposite angles. By fitting alternative guides with unequal angles the same jig can be used to produce even more complex patterns. A sliding stop or positioning marks align each subsequent groove to produce equal consecutive or grouped spac-

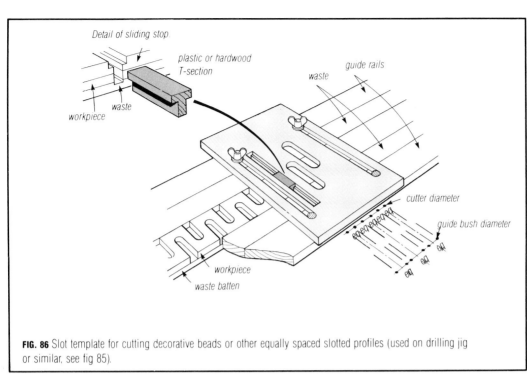

FIG. 86 Slot template for cutting decorative beads or other equally spaced slotted profiles (used on drilling jig or similar, see fig 85).

▲ **FIG. 86**

ing. To produce parallel lines the router is fed continuously against one face of the angle guide, for cross-hatching it is fed against alternate faces (see Fig. 85).

Stopped-Groove Jig

A similar sliding stop can be incorporated in a template designed to produce a series of stopped grooves, cut from alternate sides. Not only can this type of jig be used to cut decorative beads; it can also be used to great advantage when cutting indexing guides for use with other templates and jigs. To obtain maximum precision a sub-base is fitted to the router incorporating a fixed end stop and adjustable length stop (see Fig. 86).

Extrusion Jig

For commercial purposes involving repetitive cutting operations the use of a jig can offer great savings in labour costs and production time. Although purpose-made jigs to perform a specific function can be easily developed and made up by the product manufacturer, specialized combined router jigs such as the ELU SAL 54 can be used. Designed initially for the aluminium window industry, it has many applications for pre-assembly drilling and slotting of extruded non-ferrous and plastic sections.

The router motor is supported on a precision clamping frame which is fitted directly to the extrusion by the use of integral stops to accurately align it. An interchangeable metal template (cut to suit the user's requirements) is held within the frame and the router head plunged into the extrusion and locked by a quick-release knob. A sliding mount within the frame allows the router to be fed transversely and guided laterally by the template. The ELU machine jig is extremely efficient and makes possible fast and accurate setting up between operations and cutting. The ELU SAL 54 is powered by a single-phase 600 watt motor with a single running speed of 20,000 rpm. Higher wattage and more automated machines are also available. When using a variable-speed router to machine aluminium extrusions, the cutter speed should be set at around 12,000 rpm. At this and certainly at higher speeds a coolant may be required, while the use of a stick or spray lubricant will greatly improve the quality of the finished cut and extend cutter life. A range of cutters specifically designed for cutting soft aluminium, anodized aluminium and UPVC materials are available for use in these machines as well as in handheld and stationary routers (see cutter section page 30).

Curved and Shaped Work

Arched and circular work is commonly used as a decorative feature in furniture and architectural design. However, the visual effect can be easily ruined if the work is not cut to a smooth radius or curve.

By turning the router about a fixed pivot point, arcs and circles can be cut to a precise, even radius. By varying the position of the pivot point complex curves and archwork can be cut and moulded with ease.

The simplest guide for curved work is the trammel or circle-cutting guide, which consists of a rod fixed at one end to the router base with a pivot pin at the other (see Fig. 87). To enable the curve or circle radius to be altered the rod is normally slid through and secured in one of the side fence rod clamps. The pivot pin is simply pressed firmly into the centre of the workpiece and the router swung about it.

This method can be used to cut out the shape of the workpiece or to machine shallow mouldings, grooves or rebates into the surface. When making shallow relief cuts it is preferable to fit a fine depth adjuster to the router to allow the depth of cut to be set precisely. For deep cuts or when cutting completely through the material the cut should be made in several passes using the turret stop facility to increase the depth of

RIGHT Fig. 87 When cutting large diameter circles and arched work the router can be swung about a centre point set by a trammel arm held in the side fence rod clamps.

▼ **FIG. 87**

cut by 3 or 4mm on each. When cutting through the material use a straight cutter of at least 9mm diameter and lay thin hardboard or other waste material beneath the workpiece, setting the final cutter depth to cut approximately 1mm into its surface. This ensures a clean, neat edge on the under side. Having cut out a circular or curved shape, the edges can be decoratively moulded by simply substituting the straight cutter for a moulding cutter and swinging the trammel from the same centre points, or by fitting a self-guiding cutter to follow the edge contour.

To avoid costly mistakes always set out complex curves lightly on the face of the material, marking each pivot point with crossed centre lines. To avoid marking the face of the workpiece fix a small pad of plywood with double-sided tape, using the centre lines to align and transfer the pivot point.

To cut diameters less than the radius of the router base a sub-base can be attached with a centre pin fitted to it. Alternatively, an adjustable trammel point can be built into the sub-base, allowing the radius to be set as required (see Fig. 88).

When it is acceptable to fill or plug the surface of the workpiece a loose pin can be used to achieve the same effect, both the workpiece and the sub-base being drilled to take the pin (see Fig. 89). Use a pin of about 3mm diameter, projecting into the base and workpiece by at least 6mm. The hole diameter should be drilled to give a fairly tight fit. By drilling a series of holes at different radii in the sub-base and varying the pin position on the work, complex and intricate circular patterns can be obtained.

Both trammel and loose-pin methods can be used to great advantage in cutting templates from which the finished workpiece can be cut using a guide bush or self-guiding cutter. For complex patterns it is often worth cutting several templates, each to cut a different part of the pattern. This allows each template to be simplified and avoids cutting away too much material, making them less likely to distort. In a convenient position drill matching locating dowel holes to allow each template to be aligned accurately over the workpiece.

Ellipse Trammel

The ellipse jig is a variation on the single-pivot trammel and simplifies the setting out, cutting and decorative edge finishing of ellipse or oval tops and panels. The principle of the jig is to decrease the radius of the described arc in an even gradient between the major and minor axes by moving the pivot points in a controlled arc about the centre point of the ellipse. Grooves are accurately machined at 90° to each other in the jig's centre plate to take two dovetail slide blocks each fitted with pivot clamps to grip the trammel rod. The router is mounted on the trammel arm using an adaptor to fit directly into the 6 or 8mm side fence rod clamps on ELU routers or an adaptor-base where this facility is not available.

In use the major and minor axes are marked out on the workpiece and the jig plate centred over them, secured by screws or double-sided tape. With the appropriate cutter fitted, the router is positioned on the circumference of the ellipse along the minor axis and the pivot point tightened with the slide centred along the axis line. The router is then swung and the second pivot set midway along the major axis. With the router on the surface of the panel, plunge-cut to the required depth and swing the router at a constant feed speed. On thick materials cut in several steps, increasing the depth of cut for each (see Fig. 90).

The Trend ellipse jig is designed to cut ellipses with a maximum length along the major axis of 1,800mm and exact circles up to 1,670mm diameter. The maximum and minimum widths (minor axis) possible with the jig for a given length (major axis) are:

Major Axis	Minor Axis (Max)	(Min)
1800mm	1670mm	1370mm
1500mm	1370mm	1060mm
1200mm	1060mm	760mm
900mm	760mm	660mm
810mm	660mm	660mm

Any variation between these maximum and minimum widths can be produced.

To avoid leaving a centre point mark when using a circle or ellipse trammel, set out on the under side of the panel or workpiece whenever possible. Alternatively, lay thin waste plywood or hardboard over the complete panel or a pad at the centre point only. Secure with double-sided tape, and set out the centre point and axis on it.

Copy Routing

One of the latest developments in routing equipment is the copy router, which is capable of reproducing three-dimensional engraved, relief and figure forms. The Wiva-mac copying frame consists of a simple frame in which the master form and reproduction blank are held. A handwheel to the front of the frame engages via a worm gear drive in the end of the blank, allowing it to be rotated. The router motor is supported on a counterbalanced frame above the workpiece, the frame sliding freely on ball-bearing mounts along hardened-steel side

▲ FIG. 88

ABOVE Fig. 88 Small diameter circles can be cut using either an adjustable centre point carried on the side fence rods or set into a sub-base fitted to the router.

▼ FIG. 89

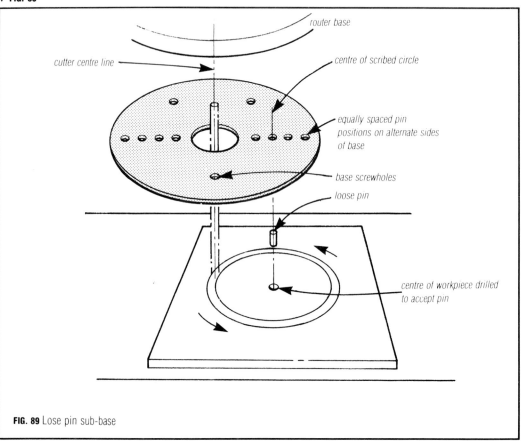

router base

cutter centre line

centre of scribed circle

equally spaced pin positions on alternate sides of base

base screwholes

loose pin

centre of workpiece drilled to accept pin

FIG. 89 Lose pin sub-base

rails. A follower and guide handle are mounted on the frame above the master form, allowing the operator to keep the tip in contact with the surface of the form as well as to slide the counterbalanced frame back and forth along the length of the workpiece (see Fig. 91). As the work is cut mainly by the tip of the cutter, only cutters with good bottom-cut characteristics should be used. By changing the cutter size and shape various surface textures can be produced.

Turned and Fluted Work

Multifaceted or fluted spindles or columns are easily cut on a box jig using a simple indexing system to divide and position the workpiece. Tapered faceted spindles can also be cut in this way. The indexing card is divided into the appropriate number of flutes, taking into consideration their depth and shape. The card is then centred and fixed to turn with the workpiece, aligning with a datum mark on the jig. With the index card and datum mark aligned the workpiece is clamped in the first facet

position, and the router support rails set parallel or at the required gradient to it. With the channel section sub-base and appropriate cutter fitted, the router is fed along the length of the workpiece, using the turret depth stop to limit the depth of cut on each pass as necessary. After the first facet or flute has been cut the work is turned to the next facet position clamped, and the process repeated. For stopped flutes, blocks or peg stops can be fitted to the router support rails (see Fig. 92).

Alternatively, the router can be used in conjunction with a lathe to perform these operations using an indexing system to position the flutes and parallel guides either side of the workpiece to carry the router (see Fig. 93).

Turning

Both parallel and tapered turned work can be produced, the work first being multifaceted as above and then trimmed by turning it against the rotating cutter by a handwheel or crank at one end of the jig (see Fig. 94). For tapered items the router support slides

ABOVE Fig. 90 The ellipse jig consists of two sliding swivels connected to the router by a single rod. The clamping position of the swivels along the rod determine the required ellipse axis lengths.

OPPOSITE Fig. 91 The principle adopted for most copy routers is to mount the router on a centrally pivoted counter balanced frame itself freely running from side to side and backwards and forwards on parallel guide rails.

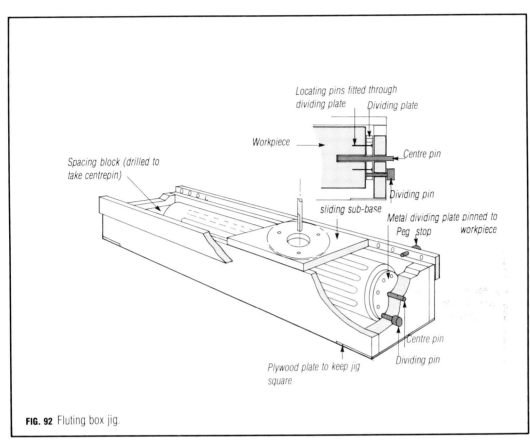

Locating pins fitted through dividing plate

Dividing plate

Workpiece

Centre pin

Spacing block (drilled to take centrepin)

Dividing pin

sliding sub-base

Metal dividing plate pinned to workpiece

Peg stop

Centre pin

Dividing pin

Plywood plate to keep jig square

FIG. 92 Fluting box jig.

◀ **FIG. 91** · ▲ **FIG. 92** · ▼ **FIG. 93**

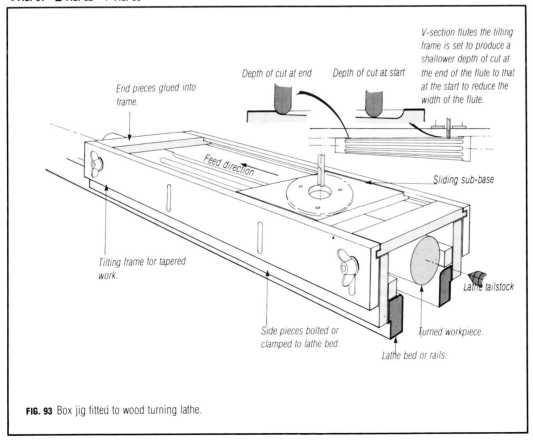

V-section flutes the tilting frame is set to produce a shallower depth of cut at the end of the flute to that at the start to reduce the width of the flute.

Depth of cut at end   Depth of cut at start

End pieces glued into frame.

Feed direction

Sliding sub-base

Tilting frame for tapered work.

Lathe tailstock

Side pieces bolted or clamped to lathe bed.

Turned workpiece.

Lathe bed or rails.

FIG. 93 Box jig fitted to wood turning lathe.

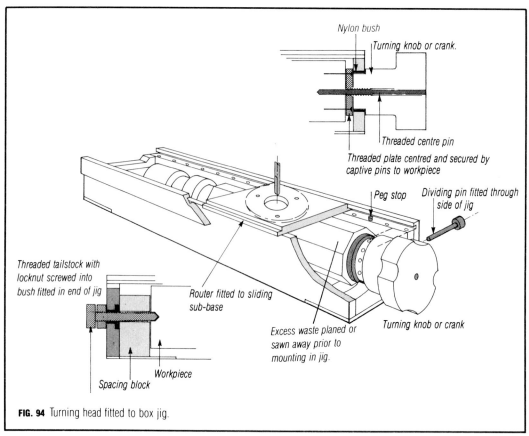

Nylon bush

Turning knob or crank.

Threaded centre pin

Threaded plate centred and secured by captive pins to workpiece

Peg stop

Dividing pin fitted through side of jig

Threaded tailstock with locknut screwed into bush fitted in end of jig

Router fitted to sliding sub-base

Excess waste planed or sawn away prior to mounting in jig.

Turning knob or crank

Spacing block

Workpiece

FIG. 94 Turning head fitted to box jig.

▲ **FIG. 94** · ▼ **FIG. 95**

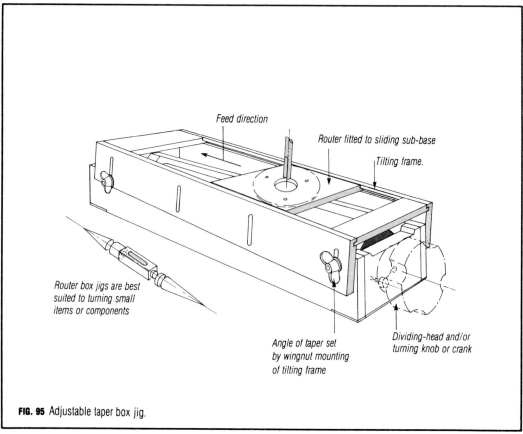

Feed direction

Router fitted to sliding sub-base

Tilting frame.

Router box jigs are best suited to turning small items or components

Angle of taper set by wingnut mounting of tilting frame

Dividing-head and/or turning knob or crank

FIG. 95 Adjustable taper box jig.

are simply set at an angle to the surface of the workpiece as before (see Fig. 95). This method can be used to cut a continuous length or short length of various cross-sectional shape along the workpiece. Use a large-diameter cutter with good bottom-cut characteristics and feed the cutter sideways into the wood at each stage before turning the workpiece. Once turned, the workpiece can then be fluted using the index system.

Decorative Mouldings

The router can be used in many ways to cut mouldings, veins, rosettes and other decorative features by means of the comprehensive range of cutters offered by machine tool

suppliers such as Trend. Many common mouldings styles such as ovolo and ogee are available in a range of standard sizes, both with or without pin or bearing pilots. Variations on these styles allow the cutter simultaneously to cut the moulding profile and square the remaining edge or trim the complete edge, leaving the moulding profile on both the top and under side at the same time (see Fig. 97). Standard variations on these profiles include cutters such as the classic style, which produces a symmetrical profile. The single cutter can be used to form both sides of decorative hinged drop-leaf or frame joints as well as edge or panel moulds. Other moulding styles are readily available for cutting new work or matching existing

▼ **FIG. 96**

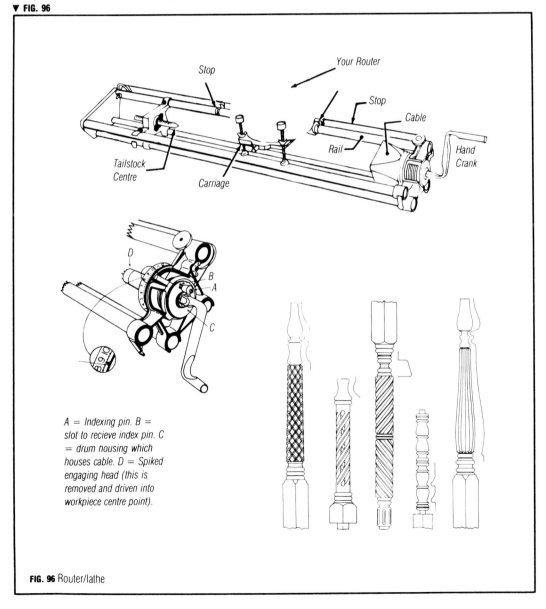

A = Indexing pin. B = slot to recieve index pin. C = drum nousing which houses cable. D = Spiked engaging head (this is removed and driven into workpiece centre point).

FIG. 96 Router/lathe

▲ FIG. 97   ▼ FIG. 98

ABOVE RIGHT Fig. 97 Decorative edge and panel mouldings can be cut using the wide range of moulding cutters which include self-guiding cutters for edge or template work and the large diameter fielded panel cutters.

ABOVE BOTTOM Fig. 98 Curved components can first be trimmed to shape using a flat template pinned or held with double-sided tape to the rough cut material and a guide bush or bearing guided cutter to follow the outline.

styles on reproduction furniture, or for architraves, picture rails and other architectural features. Cutter manufacturers and suppliers will also arrange for cutters to be ground to customers' specific profiles and/or requirements.

Multi-Cut Mouldings

Although standard ranges of profile cutters are fairly comprehensive, many more complex profiles can be produced by building up composite shapes by using one or more standard cutters, making a series of passes at different widths and depths. Not only does this offer an alternative method of matching existing furniture and architectural mouldings, using a range of inexpensive cutters; it also allows other complex shapes to be produced, such as handrail sections, drawer- and door-pull profiles and angled door and window frame mullions. The profile

guide at the back of the book shows many variations and practical uses of composite mouldings and also gives information on the cutters used to produce them.

When cutting multi-cut profiles thought must be given to the sequence in which each pass is made to ensure that adequate material is left to either guide the cutter pilot or fence or to support the base of the router level. In some cases it may be necessary to hold the workpiece in a jig or fit temporary battens to act as a guide, or to support the router either level or at an angle to the face of the workpiece (see Fig. 98).

Panel Moulds

A recent development in cutter design is large-diameter panel cutters. These are intended for producing recessed or raised panel features on cabinet doors and other solid wood or dense-particle or fibreboard (MDF, etc.) panelwork. However, because of their large diameter and therefore high peripheral speed, these cutters (those of 50mm diameter or over) should be used at a maximum shaft speed of 12,000 rpm and only in stationary inverted or overhead machines (see page 44).

Curved Mouldings

Mouldings can be applied along the edges of curved rails or panels by means of either a bearing-guided cutter or, where the surface curves in both directions, a secondary curved baseplate and curved side fence. When making up curved bases and fence blocks to follow an irregular curve, the radius of the curve should be less than that of the surface it is following and care should be taken to prevent the router rocking and to keep it at the same angle throughout the curve. If the surface curve is of an equal radius throughout the block can be cut to a matching radius (see Fig. 99).

Lettering

The manoeuvrability of the router for cutting pierced or raised carving on flat-face panel work lends itself well to the production of decorative and informative signs. Lettering, numerals and logos can be easily cut, either freehand following a pencilled

▲ FIG. 100 · ▼ FIG. 101

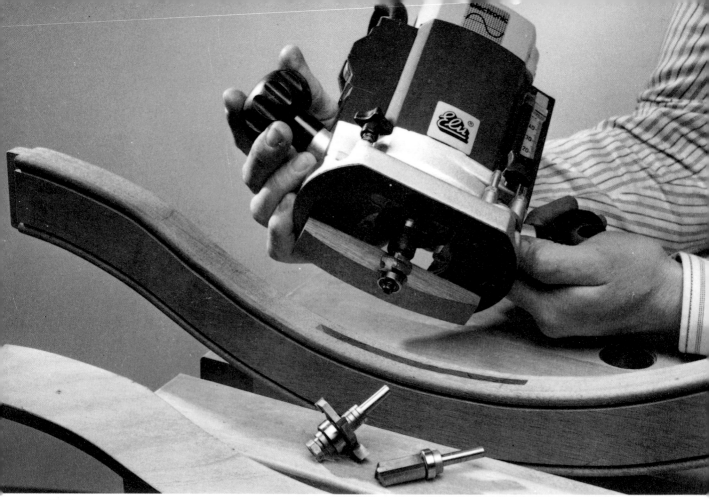

▲ **FIG. 99**

PREVIOUS PAGE, ABOVE Fig. 100 An adjustable template frame is of particular use when machining panel mouldings in the face of doors or drawer fronts or for cutting recesses or apertures.

PREVIOUS PAGE, BELOW Fig. 101 To produce various corner details using the adjustable frame template shaped inserts can be fitted into the frame as required.

ABOVE Fig. 99 To machine the decorative moulding along the edges of curved rails, a curved block can be fitted to the base of the router, keeping the router tangential to the curve throughout the cut.

outline or using pre-cut templates with a suitable guide bush. When using either method it is most important not only to achieve a good clean cut finish to the work but that the size, style and proportion of the lettering and layout are complementary. To enhance surface-engraved lettering cutters of various shapes can be used, such as radiused-end or V-point.

Setting Out Lettering

A good source of lettering styles is from graphic catalogues available from drawing office supply and art shops. These generally show a wide range of typefaces and give information on spacing and layout. Alternatively, if the economics of the job allow, many signwriting services produce computer-set and cut self-adhesive lettering in a wide range of typefaces and sizes. The former (as with examples from magazines and publicity material) can be copied directly onto the face of the work or template material either by tracing or by using a pantograph to trace and, if required enlarge, the original. The latter, which is already

correctly spaced out on the peel-off backing, can be simply transferred to thicker paper or card and cut out as a stencil, which can then be traced onto the work. When cutting the template or panel, guide the router freehand, taking great care to follow the outline precisely and smoothly. Alternatively, where the letter style is formed of straight lines, the radiused corners can be plunge-drilled and the router guided against a straight edge or set square. Lettering templates are best cut from clear plastic such as Perspex for ease of positioning. To hold a template on the workpiece use double-sided tape or a purpose-made jig (see Figs 102 and 103).

Routergraph

For commercial light engraving and copy-engraving work a pantograph-guided router can be used, such as the Trend Routergraph (see Fig. 104). The routergraph operates in a similar fashion to a drawing pantograph, with the weight of the router being supported rigidly on the pivoted arm. Precision ball-bearing pivoted linkages ensure that

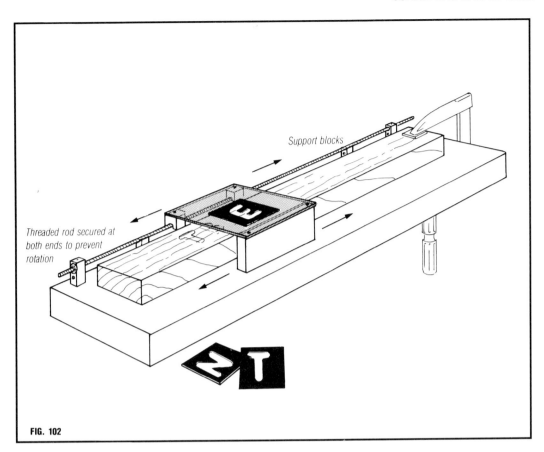

Support blocks

Threaded rod secured at both ends to prevent rotation

FIG. 102

LEFT Figs 102 and 103 This simple lettering jig uses a threaded rod to position the template frame. Proprietary or purpose-made letter templates can then be laid in the frame, the weight of the router holding both in position while cutting.

▲ **FIG. 102** · ▼ **FIG. 103**

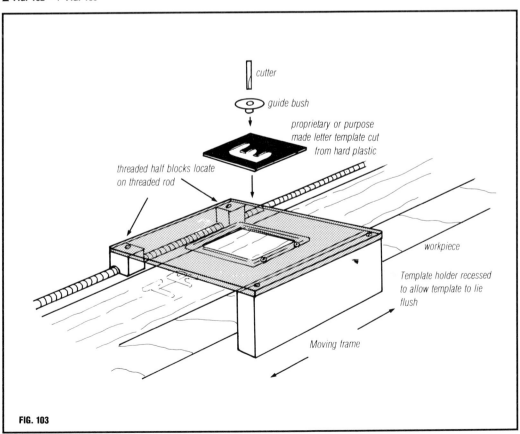

cutter

guide bush

proprietary or purpose made letter template cut from hard plastic

threaded half blocks locate on threaded rod

workpiece

Template holder recessed to allow template to lie flush

Moving frame

FIG. 103

ABOVE Fig. 104 An overarm pantograph such as the Trend Routergraph offers the facility to copy (1:1 ratio) directly from pre-cut templates or flat artwork to cut nameplates, signs and other relief or recessed work.

OPPOSITE Fig. 105 The handheld router can be used for freehand carving and relief work on name boards, numbers, and other craftwork. The design is first traced onto the material and the outline cut in steps before removing the waste.

Safety Tip

Regularly check the condition of the router and accessories and have any worn or damaged parts replaced.

the router cutter follows smoothly and precisely the path traced by a stylus or template follower pin over the original master or template. Pins are available in various diameters to suit the cutter diameter being used. The routergraph can be mounted on a flat work surface or on the optional baseboard (Trend), which has inset scales graduated in both metric and imperial. To assist in positioning and holding the workpiece optional cross-alignment bars with graduated scales inset along one edge are designed to clamp across the baseboard.

Ready-cut pierced letter templates are available for the routergraph in Goudy Bold (87mm high), Old English (87mm) and block upper and lower case typefaces (25mm, 38mm, 50mm and 75mm) and as raised templates for relief carving or cutting separate letters in Helvetica (75mm), Barnum (50mm and 75mm), and Jubilee (50, 75 and 100mm). Also available are raised-end frame templates, which are used to cut decorative ends on signs and nameplates. To position and hold the letter templates, a carrier frame is available which will accept up to two rows of 75mm-high lettering templates, and can also be used to hold

purpose-made templates and patterns. The routergraph is capable of copying and cutting rectangular work up to 250mm × 300mm and 450mm × 150mm, and circular work up to 360mm diameter.

Freehand Work

Freehand use of the router is often thought to be restricted to surface relief carving in the production of decorative patterns, lettering for nameplates, and three-dimensional carving. However, in practice the router can be used in much the same way as a portable jigsaw in scribing to fit or to cut apertures in panelling, firestop materials, and other sheet cladding products, to accommodate ductwork, steelwork, pipes and electrical services. The main benefit of using the router as opposed to the jigsaw is that it ensures a clean square cut and is often more manoeuvrable when working in confined spaces.

To use the plunge router freehand, that is without a guide attachment or self-guiding cutter, for general cutting operations requires little practice, whereas intricate work in natural timbers requires some experience in understanding the characteristics of the wood itself. As the router will cut in any direction in which it is fed (a jigsaw blade cannot cut sideways) it is susceptible to any directional pressure. If the hardness of the wood changes along the cut (from hard grain to sapwood) the side pressure required to keep the cutter against the cutting face alters, causing a tendency for it to be pulled or thrown off line. Therefore, as when using any hand-guided tool, only the skill and concentration of the woodworker can ensure a good standard of work.

In freehand cutting the side pressures on the cutter tend to be more erratic and variable than when following a controlled path, increasing the strain and therefore the risk of cutter breakage. For this reason the depth of cut in relation to the diameter of the cutter should be limited to slightly less than for guided work, with the full depth being achieved in steps of no more than 2 or 3mm. When possible, remove as much material as possible from the waste areas before finishing with a very fine trimming cut to full depth along the border or contour

▲ FIG. 105

line. This avoids step marks and the need to overtrim the line to remove them. For narrow lines and veining cuts it may be necessary to cut to the full depth in one step, which, for cutters below 6mm in diameter, should be restricted to a similar dimension.

In freehand routing care should be taken in the way the machine is held, since most of the operator's concentration will need to be on what the cutter is doing. In intricate work there is a tendency to guide the router by the base, leaving the fingers very close and exposed to the cutter. In this situation, which gives more precise control (but omits use of the plunge action), it is better to fit a small sub-base with side handles to give a positive grip while still guiding the router from low down. For heavier work the router should always be held by the side handles, or one side handle and the base handle when an extension sub-base is fitted.

9 | Drilling, Boring and Dowelling

The plunge action of most modern routers ensures that the cutter enters the workpiece at precisely 90° to the surface while the high cutting speed leaves a clean, sharp, straight hole, a facility that lends itself ideally to many drilling and boring applications.

Most two-flute cutters now available are designed for plunge cutting into most materials, including natural timbers and resin-bonded boards, though for repetitive drilling in these materials up to 8mm diameter solid carbide cutters are most suited. For holes over 8mm diameter two-flute cutters with a centre tip are to be preferred (see Cutters, page 37). For drilling materials such as anodized aluminium, UPVC and special cutters are available (see page 36).

Alternatively, when using routers fitted with variable speed control or in conjunction with a separate speed control unit, twist drills and dowel drills with reduced shank diameters to fit the standard router collets can be used at an appropriate speed.

Also available for plunge boring are hinge-sinking cutters for fitting round-boss concealed cabinet hinges, and a range of screw countersinks, counterbores and plug cutters (see Fig. 106).

To ensure a fast clean cutting action and to eliminate the risk of leaving burn marks on the work, good chip clearance must be maintained and the correct speed must be selected to suit both the cutter type and the material being worked. Cutters above 25mm may need to be plunged into the material in several stages, cutting to a depth of 9–12mm on each, bringing the tip up almost but not completely out of the hole to allow the waste material to clear from round the flutes. Large-diameter cutters of this size and cutters such as the hinge-sink type should be used at speeds of about 10,000 rpm. Smaller-diameter router cutters can be used at progressively faster speeds, with those 6mm or less running at maximum router speed (from 28,000 to 30,000 rpm). However, drill bits, countersinks and other special cutters should be used only at the manufacturers' recommended speed.

The plunge router is best suited to drilling and boring at right angles to the surface of the workpiece, the base sitting firmly on it. For angled holes it is necessary to make up a jig to support the router or to hold the workpiece at the required angle to it (see Fig. 107).

A common problem when using the router for plunge drilling is the tendency, especially on slippery surfaces, for the turning motion of the cutter as it bites into the surface to jog the router slightly, resulting in an oval start to the hole or damage across the surface of the workpiece. This can be avoided by fixing fine abrasive paper to the base with double-sided tape when working natural timber or man-made board. When working on finished, polished or hard surfaces, soft rubber pads can be used, for example the rubber patches from a tyre repair kit.

For accurate work it is necessary to be able to centre the cutter precisely and there are several methods of achieving this. The simplest is to score points inside the router base to define the crossed centre lines of the cutter (see Fig. 108). Alternatively, the

▲ FIG. 106 · ▼ FIG. 107

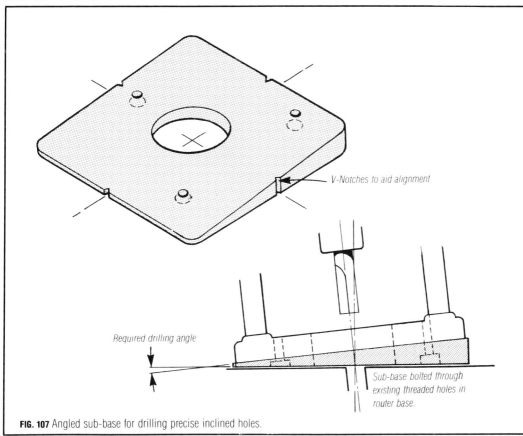

ABOVE Fig. 106 The precision of the plunge action router lends itself well to screw sinking and counterboring operations. A full range of screwsinks and counterbores are available as well as a range of matching plug cutters.

V-Notches to aid alignment

Required drilling angle

Sub-base bolted through existing threaded holes in router base.

FIG. 107 Angled sub-base for drilling precise inclined holes.

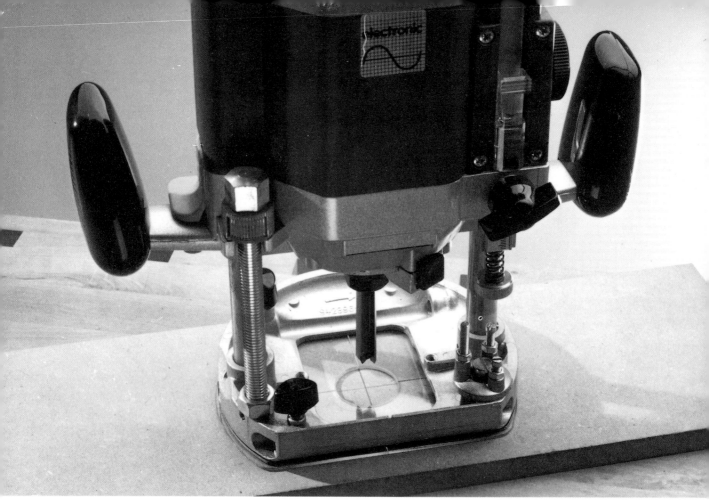

▲ FIG. 108

router base can be replaced with a clear Perspex base or have a clear false base fixed over it with double-sided tape. With a V-cut or other pointed cutter, mark the centre by lightly plunge-drilling the clear Perspex with the tip. Engrave crossed centre lines at 90° to each other on the under side of the base (these can be filled with black enamel paint for clarity). Drill out the centre hole (to allow swarf to clear) using a large-diameter cutter. In either case, to centre the router mark the centre point of the hole on the surface of the workpiece and draw fine crossed centre lines through it. Align the centre lines on the router base with those on the workpiece.

Plug Cutters, Countersinks and Counterbores

These are traditional methods of disguising screws and other fastenings as well as small knots and other surface blemishes. The counterbore drills a clean precise hole into which the fastening head is sunk or with which the blemish is taken out. A plug, the same diameter as the hole, is then cut from matching timber with a cutter of similar size and glued into the hole. By careful matching of grain and colour, tapping the precisely fitting plug into the hole, and trimming the protruding plug level with the surface, a near-invisible finish can be achieved. Counterbores for sinking screws are designed to cut the shank hole and, when using countersunk-headed screws, the countersink as well as the bore for the plug all in one operation. They are available in various sizes to suit specific screw gauges (Trend supply them for No. 8, 10 and 12 gauge screws). Fitted with lip and spur solid carbide tips they can be used at speeds between 1,000 and 20,000 rpm (see Fig. 106).

Hinge Sinkers

Concealed cabinet hinges having a round boss set into the face of the workpiece are commonly used in the construction of fitted units and freestanding furniture. To ensure that the door or flap is held rigidly, the hinge bosses must be a tight press fit in the holes. To achieve this the holes must be drilled clean and precise, and carefully aligned in

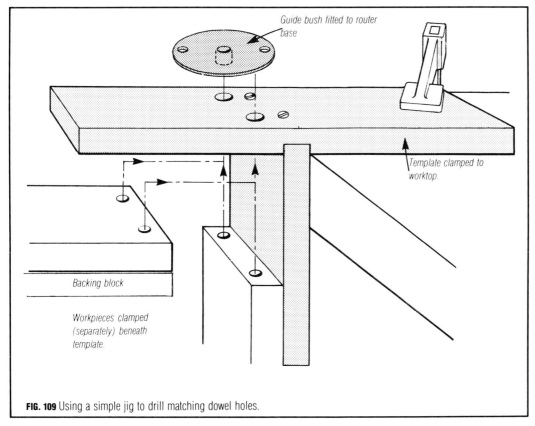

Guide bush fitted to router base

Template clamped to worktop.

Backing block

Workpieces clamped (separately) beneath template.

FIG. 109 Using a simple jig to drill matching dowel holes.

▲ **FIG. 109**

relation to the edge of the panel. Hinges are available in five standard sizes, 20, 25, 26, 30 and 35mm diameter; 26 and 35mm are the two most commonly used. Hinge sinkers (see Fig. 106) are generally available in all sizes and in various flute configurations to suit different materials, such as plastic-laminate-faced particle board and natural timbers. Economically priced general-purpose cutters are also available (offered by Trend in 35mm diameter only). Because of the type of materials they are likely to be used on and the need for them to make precise cuts consistently, tungsten-carbide-tipped cutters are essential. Cutting speeds for cutters of 25mm and over should be restricted to between 1,000 and 10,000 rpm to avoid burning. To align the cutter quickly and accurately a template can be used to position the router the required distance in from the edges of the panel or stile.

Templates can also be used to position holes for fittings such as basin taps set into worktops or vanity units, the hole being drilled with a suitably sized hinged sink cutter centred through a large-diameter

guide bush. Large-diameter holes plunge-cut with the router in this way are clean-cut with no edge chipping, as often occurs when drilling holes through laminate-faced boards.

Dowel Joints

Dowel jointing can be effectively carried out using the router in conjunction with simple jigs or a more universal indexing system. Most dowelling jigs are fairly basic, utilizing a standard guide bush to centre the cutter in predrilled template holes spaced to provide optimum strength between the joint faces (see Fig. 109). Pre-cut dowels are available in various lengths and diameters to match to standard straight cutter and dowel drill sizes. By fitting stops to the jig, matching components can be drilled quickly and accurately to ensure perfect alignment of the dowel holes. Dowels can also be used to strengthen corner mitre joints, a similar jig as for right-angled dowel joints being used, clamped with the template against the angled faces of the mitre in turn. When dowel-jointing wide boards to form either

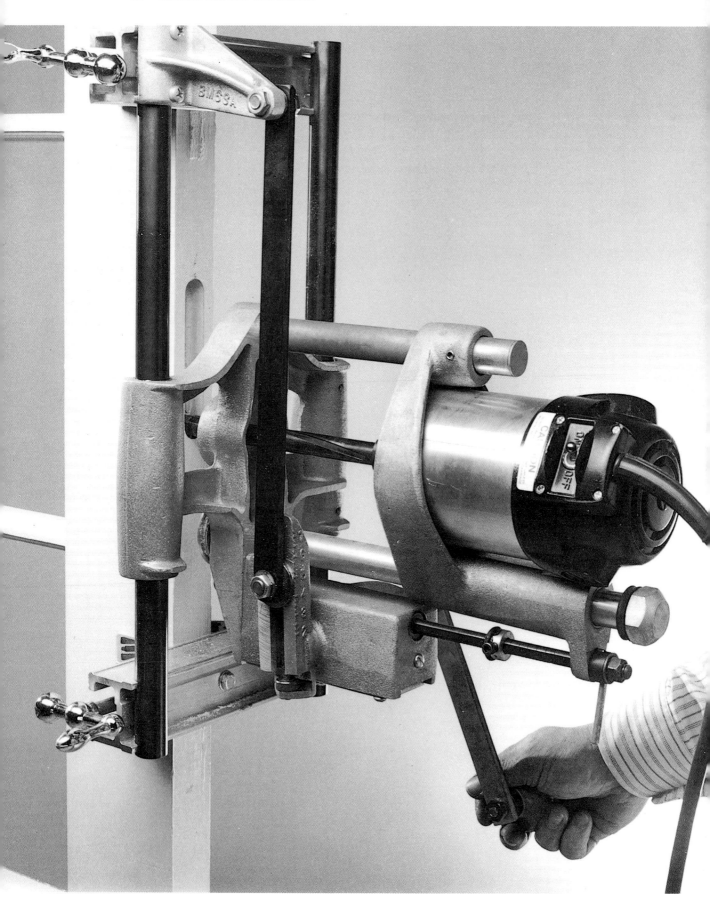

◄ **FIG. 111** · ▲ **FIG. 110** · ▼ **FIG. 113**

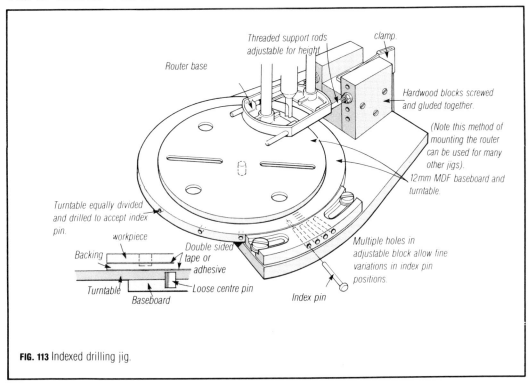

Threaded support rods
adjustable for height

clamp.

Router base

Hardwood blocks screwed
and glued together.

(Note this method of
mounting the router
can be used for many
other jigs).

12mm MDF baseboard and
turntable.

Turntable equally divided
and drilled to accept index
pin.

workpiece

Backing

Double sided
tape or
adhesive

Turntable

Loose centre pin

Baseboard

Multiple holes in
adjustable block allow fine
variations in index pin
positions.

Index pin

FIG. 113 Indexed drilling jig.

*OPPOSITE Fig. 111
Primarily designed for
the fast fitting of mortise
locks, the mortising
router automatically
centres and cuts the
mortise in steps to a
pre-set depth.*

*ABOVE Fig. 110
Dowel positions can be
accurately set out using
a simple indexing
system consisting of a
perforated strip set into
a straight edge, a pin on
the router base locating
in the strip at the
required spacing.*

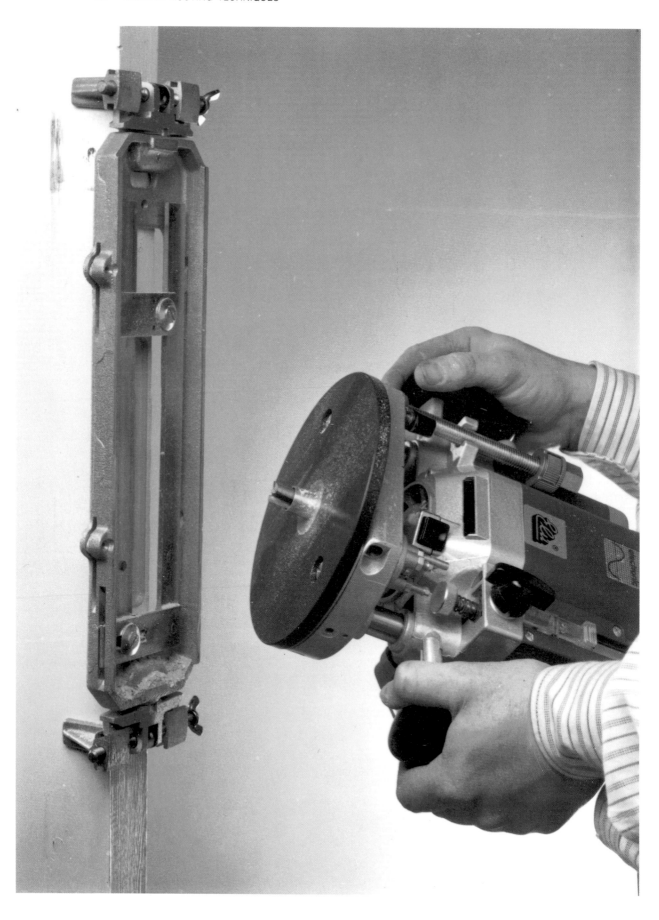

right-angle or T-joints, an indexing strip can be used. The two pieces to be joined are clamped vertically and horizontally to a simple machining table (see page 107), their front edges butted against a common stop. The indexing strip, which may be a length of any rigid material with close equally spaced holes (such as perforated metal strapping used in building construction), is fixed to a straight edge used to clamp the horizontal panel to the table. An indexing pin fitted to the base of the router locates in the holes, positioning the router ready to plunge-cut the dowel hole. By marking the required dowel spacings for easy reference and setting the straight edge parallel to the edge of the board, each line of matching dowel holes can be drilled in the face of the horizontal board or centred along the edge of the vertical one.

Curved Surfaces

For drilling into round or curved sections, or along the arris of a triangular section, saddle or V-blocks can be made up to sit over the section and support the router level. Such blocks are drilled to locate a guide bush to centralize the cutter (see Fig. 113).

The plunge-drilling facility also offers the opportunity to create various decorative effects by means of square, round-end, V-cut or other moulding cutters which cut dimples, rosettes, flutes or peg holes. Use a template to space the decoration equally; if working freehand, sketch in the design on the workpiece or trace it on the surface of the workpiece from a stencil or pattern (see Fig. 114).

OPPOSITE Fig. 112
To complete the lock installation a shallow recess is cut using an adjustable template guide to take the lock plate.

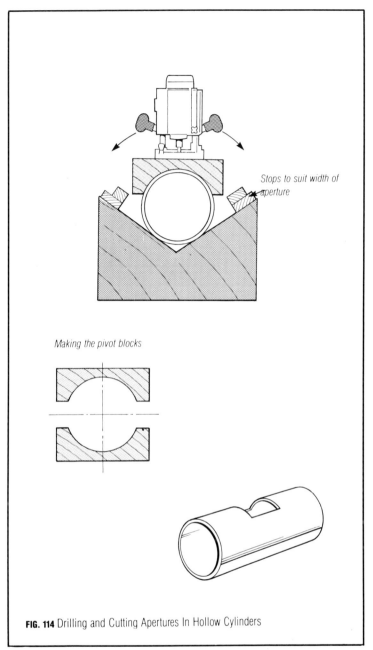

Stops to suit width of aperture

Making the pivot blocks

FIG. 114 Drilling and Cutting Apertures In Hollow Cylinders

▲ **FIG. 114**

◄ **FIG. 112**

10 | Trimming and Cutting Plastic Laminates

One specialized area in which the router has proved invaluable is the cutting and trimming of plastic laminates. Its high cutting speed ensures clean, precise edges virtually unattainable by traditional hand-finishing techniques.

Decorative plastic laminates are generally used as a facing material bonded to a thicker stable sheet material such as man-made particle-, fibre- and laminated timber-boards, preferably with a second balancing laminate (to prevent curling) bonded to the reverse side. The router can be used to cut and trim laminate sheet prior to it being bonded to the base material, or both materials can be trimmed or cut to shape together. Laminates can also be used as decorative inlays set flush into natural timber or other laminate surfaces, using the router to cut the inlay precisely to shape and to recess the background to receive it.

In most cases the normal methods of guiding the router can be used, such as with the side fence, against a straight edge, and or templates and guide bushes. Alternative methods have been developed specifically for trimming laminates. These include lateral roller guides for following regular or irregular curved surfaces, such as oval and scalloped table tops, and special trimming and combination cutters, either self-guiding or for use with guide attachments.

Self-guiding cutters are of particular use in working with laminates, particularly flush-edge trimming. However, as solid fixed pilot pins can tend to burn and mark the face of the laminate or work surface, bearing-guided cutters are to be preferred.

Plastic laminate, being a resin-based material, can be extremely damaging to cutters and only tungsten-carbide-tipped or solid-tungsten cutters are recommended. However, one problem often encountered with cutters when trimming laminates is that the cutting edges and guide bearing become coated with the bonding adhesive, which results in overheating of the cutter, which softens the adhesive and tends to make the matter worse, leaving a poor, uneven finish. This can best be avoided by cleaning cutters and bearings after use with adhesive solvent and then lightly oiling them, removing excess adhesive from the work, and ensuring that the adhesive has set and hardened before attempting to trim.

Cutter life can be further extended by avoiding unnecessary wear by reducing the edge overhang of laminates prior to trimming to no more than 3mm. Wear should also be evenly spread along the full length of the cutting edges by regularly adjusting the depth of the cutter when trimming panel edges or long runs.

Trimming Vertical Edges

It is normal practice to apply the narrow vertical edge laminate first, allowing the top face laminate to be trimmed flush with its outer face, the joint line then appearing on the edge of the workpiece rather than the top face. This also eliminates any risk of the top laminate being damaged by the bottom cutting edges as they would be skimming flush over the surface of the laminate. Initially the edging laminate should stand proud above the face of the board by no

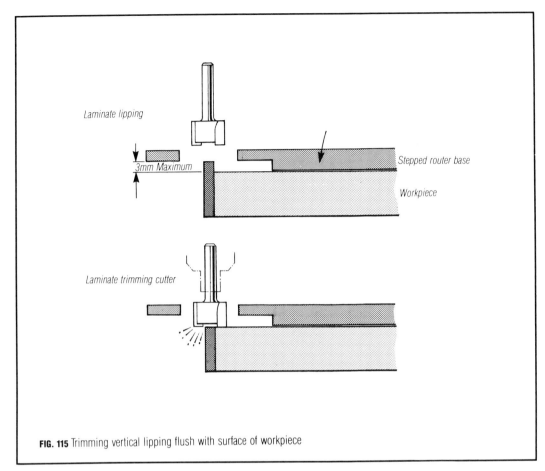

FIG. 115 Trimming vertical lipping flush with surface of workpiece

Laminate lipping

3mm Maximum

Stepped router base

Workpiece

Laminate trimming cutter

▲ **FIG. 115**

more than 3mm, a slightly thicker pad being fitted to the base of the router to clear this projection, allowing it to pass under the router base in front of the cutter (see Fig. 115). Either the pad can be held with double-sided tape to the under side of the standard base or, preferably, a wide stepped sub-base can be fitted, which also ensures better balance of the router, reducing the risk of it tipping and cutting unevenly into the top edge of the board and laminate.

Place the router on a hard flat surface and bring the under side of the cutter lightly into contact with the surface using a fine depth adjuster. Transfer the router to the work-piece and centre the cutter over the project-ing laminate, using the side fence with the fine adjuster fitted or a lateral roller guide to centre the TCT cutter over the vertical laminate. Feed the router in a clockwise direction to prevent chipping out on the decorative face of the laminate. Generally, it is possible to trim in one pass, though some qualities of laminate are more brittle and

more liable to chipping out than others, and may require to be trimmed in two or more passes, the last being a very fine skimming cut. It is often well worth taking time to produce a part sample of the workpiece and use it to set up the router initially, make trial cuts, and readjust as necessary.

Trimming Horizontal Edges

Whether the edge of the workpiece has been lipped or is to be left plain, the top-surface laminate should be cut slightly oversize and applied with approximately 3mm overhang all round. Remove as much of the excess adhesive from beneath the overhang as possible and allow it to harden, otherwise it will hinder the cutter and affect the quality of the finished edge. For trimming straight edges at 90°, the square edged trimming cutter can again be used, guided by the side fence. To ensure that the cutter does not cut into the face of the vertical-edge laminate, the side fence must be very precisely set by the fine adjuster fitted to the side fence. The

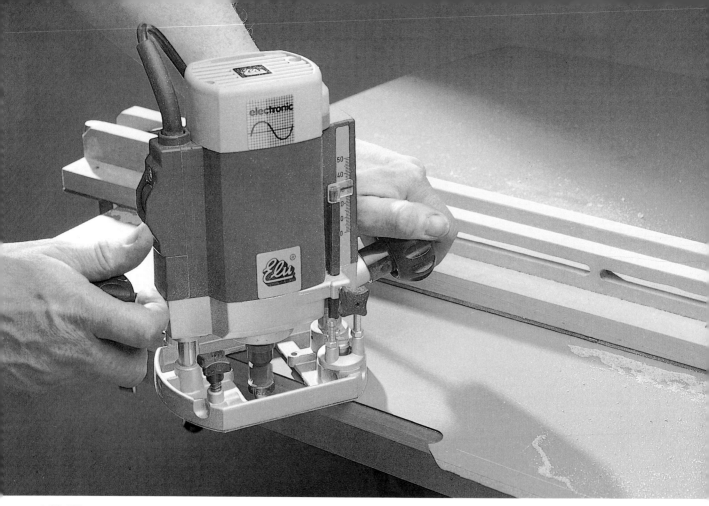

ABOVE Fig. 116 Trimming plastic laminates has been greatly simplified by the use of self-guiding TCT trimming cutters. When using bearing guided cutters always leave the adhesive to harden completely to avoid jamming the guide bearing.

direction of feed in this case is in the opposite direction to that in which the cutter is rotating, as is normal when edge routing (see Fig. 116).

Because of the hardness of plastic laminates and the precision of a router-cut edge, a sharp arris is produced which can be dangerous if left on table edges and the like. This arris should be removed with a fine-grade abrasive paper held taut across a flat sanding block.

As an alternative, the edges can be bevelled, which also has the effect of widening the edge line (the width and colour of the exposed laminate core). This can be achieved with a bevel-trimming cutter. These are designed to bevel angles at 30°, 60° and 80° when guided by the side fence, or with a template guide bush or as bearing-guided cutters, at 30°, 45°, 60°, and 80°. Combination bevel cutters are also available. These are capable of trimming the verical edge laminate as well as cutting a bevel on the face laminate, or they can be used to cut a 45° and 90° bevel or a 60° and 90° bevel by raising or lowering the cutter to use the relevant cutting edge (see Fig. 117). Bearing-guided cutters are generally used when trimming the laminate edge of regular and irregular curved or shaped surfaces, the rounded internal corners left by the cutter being squared up and finished by hand. A bearing-guided cutter can be used equally well to trim straight edges, but in both cases it will follow the edge precisely, any slight undulation in the surface of the edge laminate (due to an uneven adhesive layer beneath the laminate or poor edge finishing) will be reproduced in the finished laminate edge. Panel edges must therefore be finished as smooth and square as possible.

Whichever method of guiding the cutter is used, the base of the router must be kept flat on the surface of the laminate and it is recommended that an extension sub-base is fitted to extend the width of the router base. Where panels are faced on both sides the two edges can be trimmed simultaneously with a two-section cutter with the guide bearing fitted between them (see Fig. 118). Alternatively, when trimming double-faced straight-sided panels, the side-fence face

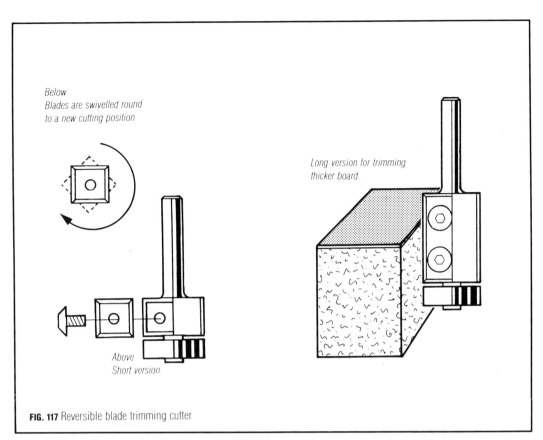

LEFT Fig. 117   *There are a number of cutters designed specifically for trimming plastic laminates including those with tungsten replaceable blades that can be swivelled through 90° to present a new cutting edge.*

Below
Blades are swivelled round to a new cutting position

Long version for trimming thicker board.

Above
Short version

FIG. 117 Reversible blade trimming cutter

▲ **FIG. 117** · ▼ **FIG. 118**

BELOW Fig. 118
Where both faces of the workpiece have been faced with laminate, both edges can be trimmed flush together using a centre bearing trimming cutter.

▲ FIG. 119

*ABOVE Fig. 119
Alternatively the side
fence can be used when
trimming laminates and
provision is made on
the ELU side fence (ELU
96 range) to turn the
face linings to give a
narrow edge to run
between the laminate
faces.*

lining on some routers such as ELU 96 and 96E models can be reversed to provide a narrow edge guide which can run between the projecting laminate edges (see Fig. 119).

Laminate-faced tables and other panels can be attractively finished with a decorative edge moulding, the exposed edges of timber-based materials often being finished in a contrasting painted or stained finish. Bearing-guided TCT profile cutters can be used for this purpose, either singly or in a multi-cut role.

Combination Trimming and Slotting

A common method of finishing panel edges in the production of utility furniture and partitioning is to cut a central slot to take a T-section plastic or metal edging strip. Using a combination cutter consisting of a straight cutter with a narrow grooving (slotter) blade fitted beneath it, the laminate edge can be trimmed flush with the edge of the panel and the slot cut simultaneously (see Fig. 120). The thickness of the blade should be slightly less than the tongue of the trim to achieve a tight fit, but take care, particularly

if the tongue is keyed or barbed, not to force the low-density core of lower-grade particle boards apart as this will show as a slightly raised edge round the panel.

Cutouts for Sinks, Hobs and Other Inset Items

There are two methods of performing this operation. The first, which is to be preferred, is to cut the aperture through the base material before applying the laminate. The second, which is often necessary for site installation of fitted worktops and vanity units, is to position and cut the opening through the pre-faced board. The first method can be best achieved by using a pierce-and-trim cutter with a drill-point tip and solid end pilot. Position the router over the aperture slightly away from the edge and use the plunge action to drill through the laminate and lower the cutter until the cutting edge is against the laminate. Cut towards the edge of the aperture until the end pilot is against it and continue cutting, with slight pressure keeping the pilot in contact and maintaining an even feed in the

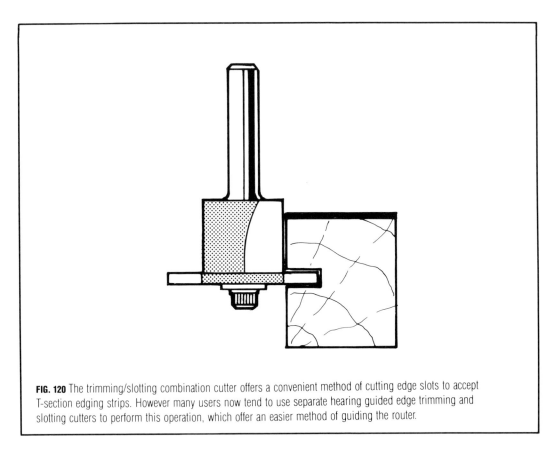

FIG. 120 The trimming/slotting combination cutter offers a convenient method of cutting edge slots to accept T-section edging strips. However many users now tend to use separate bearing guided edge trimming and slotting cutters to perform this operation, which offer an easier method of guiding the router.

▲ **FIG. 120**

opposite direction to the rotation of the cutter (see Fig. 121).

The best method of positioning and cutting apertures through pre-faced materials is to use a template which can be set out and checked for fit against the item to be inset. With most hobs, sinks, and similar items a paper template is provided by the manufacturer, which can be transferred to 6mm-thick router template material, allowing for the guide-bush margin. Holes for mounting taps and other fittings can also be positioned and cut on the same template, which can first be used to check clearances for pipework or for the under side of the inset item to sit in the frame or unit carcase beneath the worktop. Cut the opening using a large diameter (10–12mm) TCT straight cutter guided by the guide bush fitted to the router base. Support the board clear of the work surface or lay it over flat waste material that can be cut into. Position and secure the template over the board and cut in several passes, depending on the thickness of the material.

Having cut inset apertures, finish both edges with a slight bevel using a 45° cutter to remove the sharp arris to avoid chipping the laminate while the item is being fitted. With ceramic, fibreglass and pressed-metal items this bevel can be increased to allow clearance for the radiused corner of the casting or pressing, allowing it to sit snugly in the aperture flush to the surface of the laminate.

Postform Jig Template

The jointing of postformed laminate-faced worktops is an essential operation in the installation of fitted kitchens and bathrooms/vanity tops. But unchipped close-scribed edges are extremely difficult to cut by hand and just as difficult to align even if the edges are trimmed with a square-cut router cutter. To overcome this problem a postform template guide can be used (available from Trend), designed to cut a precise line at 45° across the bullnose or bevelled front edge and then to turn the cutter through a further 45° to cut a straight square face either parallel to (right-angle joint) or at any other angle (out-of-square joint) to the front edge of the worktop. A matching

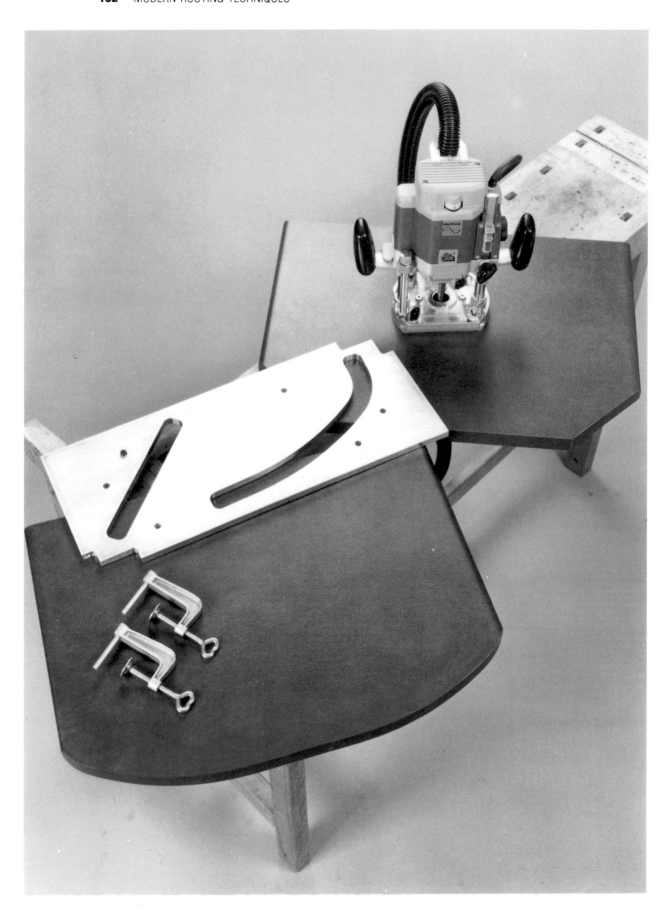

◄ FIG. 123 · ▲ FIG. 122 · ▼ FIG. 121

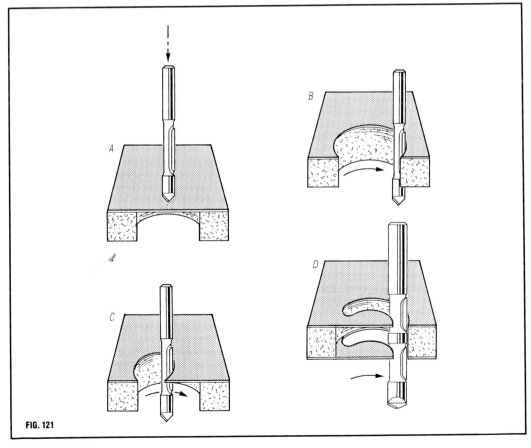

FIG. 121

OPPOSITE Fig. 123
Also available from
Trend is a template
designed to either radius
or angle the corners of
worktops when forming
island or peninsular
units, to produce a safer
and neater finish as
opposed to square
corners.

ABOVE Fig. 122   The
Trend postform jig is
designed for on-site
installation of fitted
laminate faced worktops
and allows precise
unobtrusive joints either
at 90° or to allow for
variations where wall
surfaces are out of
square.

LEFT Fig. 121   Pierce
and trim cutters are
available in several sizes
either Tungsten carbide
tipped or, for better
durability, solid carbide.

RIGHT Fig. 124 A recent introduction by Trend is a range of cutters fitted with nylon sleeved bearings designed for working and trimming solid plastic materials such as 'Corian'.

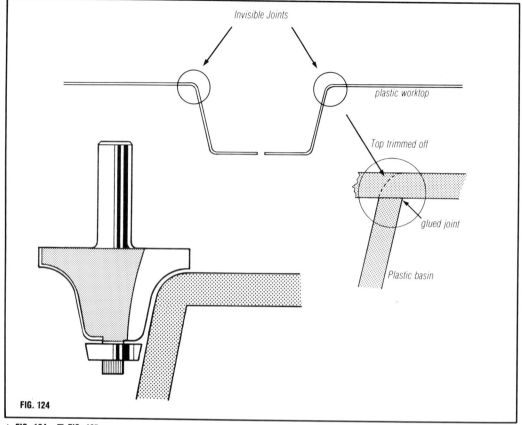

Invisible Joints

plastic worktop

Top trimmed off

glued joint

Plastic basin

FIG. 124

▲ **FIG. 124** · ▼ **FIG. 125**

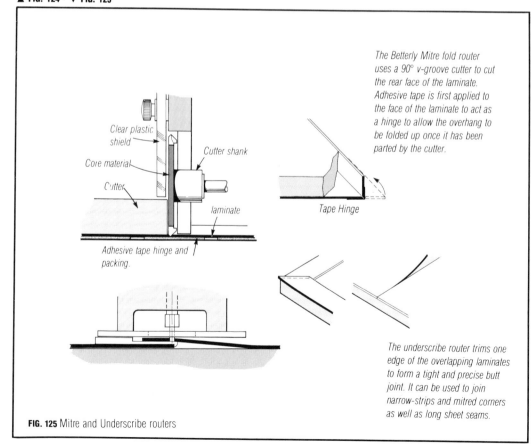

The Betterly Mitre fold router uses a 90° v-groove cutter to cut the rear face of the laminate. Adhesive tape is first applied to the face of the laminate to act as a hinge to allow the overhang to be folded up once it has been parted by the cutter.

Clear plastic shield

Cutter shank

Core material

Cutter

laminate

Adhesive tape hinge and packing.

Tape Hinge

The underscribe router trims one edge of the overlapping laminates to form a tight and precise butt joint. It can be used to join narrow-strips and mitred corners as well as long sheet seams.

FIG. 125 Mitre and Underscribe routers

template is used to cut the reverse shape on the end of the abutting section. The template kit consists of male and female templates, bolt recess template, two G-clamps, spacer bushes, Allen key and a convenient carrying case. Two sizes are available for joining worktop widths of 600, 640, and 650mm, and for worktops up to 1,000mm. However, it is possible to join 1,000mm tops to tops 600, 640, and 650mm wide with the smaller jig as long as the female profile is cut into the edge of the 1,000mm board (see Figs 122 and 123).

Solid Worktops

A new range of cutters specifically designed to cut and trim solid plastic resin, stain and scratch resistant worktop materials such as Corian (DuPont), Avointe (3–M) and 2000X (Formica), have been developed and are now available through Trend. Consisting of TCT cutters machined to specific profiles they are fitted with nylon guide bearings to prevent scratching the plastic surface. A particular use of these cutters is for trimming the openings for under-mounted basins and sinks, the bowl being glued with a special adhesive beneath a rough cut hole in the worktop. The bearing guided cutter is then used to trim the opening leaving the exposed edge of the worktop at a flush precise angle, square or rounded over, into the bowl or as a bullnose edge detail. These materials are ideal for worktops, vanity units and other surfaces being non-porous, resistant to crazing, cracking, heat and mild abrasives. As the colour or pattern goes right through the material they can be machined and finished with the router using TCT, Solid carbide, or HSSE cutters (see Fig. 124).

▲ **FIG. 126**

ABOVE Fig. 126
Trimming cutters can also be used to trim real wood veneers or trimming cut edges of veneered board. Bearing guided trimming cutters are particularly useful when trimming veneered curved or irregular edges.

11 | Woodworking Joints

OPPOSITE ABOVE
Fig. 127 Matching
tenons or halvings can
be cut together by
clamping them beneath
a straight edge which
also guides the router. A
batten laid against the
guide edge facilitates
cutting joints wider than
the cutter diameter.

OPPOSITE BELOW
Fig. 128 A simple and
inexpensive machining
table facilitates a wide
range of jointing,
trimming and moulding
operations. The table
shown incorporates drop
end and front stops and
a clamping straight edge
to hold the work.

Safety Tip

Avoid using hinges
or catches to secure
box type jigs unless
they are let flush
into the surface and
all edges are
smooth and
rounded, this can
avoid personal
injury when
handling or feeding
the router across
them.

The strength and stability of any timber structure depends largely on the precision with which the joints are both cut and assembled, as does the appearance and quality of the finished workpiece. The appearance can often be further enhanced by displaying that precision, clearly defining the joint profile as an integral feature in its visual design.

To maintain a repetitive standard when machining joints, the router can be used in combination with jigs, templates and jointing cutters, the latter being designed to produce a specific joint profile such as a mitre, a finger joint, and tongue-and-groove joints (see pages 143 and 161).

Intricate joints such as through and secret dovetails require very exact jig tolerances and are best cut on a commercially produced jig. Most other joint-making jigs and templates can be easily produced in the workshop.

Most woodworking joints are formed from a combination of two common woodworking operations, grooving and rebating, there being little difference in setting up the router to cut a wide rebate to form one side of a tenon or cutting a halving joint. The same process is simply repeated one or more times. When designing a jig or template it is therefore worth making it capable of being adjusted to suit timber sections of various sizes, and adjustable for depth of cut. To ensure uniformity in the sizing of components and the positioning of joints, and to save on the setting-up time, it is also worth making it capable of cutting several similar components at the same time.

Tenons and Halvings

There are many ways of cutting tenons and halvings. The simplest is to square the end of the timber before clamping it under a batten with the ends flush to the bench edge. Use a lead in batten to support the router as it enters the cut and a wide stop to keep it level as it leaves, and to prevent breakout. The depth and width of cut can then be set by adjusting the depth stop and side fence respectively (see Fig. 127). Similarly, several rails or components can be cut by laying them side by side, aligning the ends against a straight edge. A variation on this is to make up a machining table with adjustable end and front stops (see Fig. 128). To cut the second face of a tenon, turn the timber over and repeat the operation to the required depth. When cutting the second face of thin tenons, support the cut face on a batten as any flexing caused by the weight or vibration of the router will result in a tapered tenon (see Fig. 129).

Box jigs and tenoning boards are often used to make this type of cut, but are often limited in the size of the tenon or halving that can be cut. However, they are generally designed to allow the workpiece to be quickly and accurately positioned and, with a template or parallel guides, avoid the need to adjust the side fence to increase the width of the cut.

Tenons and halvings can be easily and successfully cut on the router table, the timber being held against the sliding bevel fence and slid over the cutter held in the inverted router. This operation is covered further on page 51.

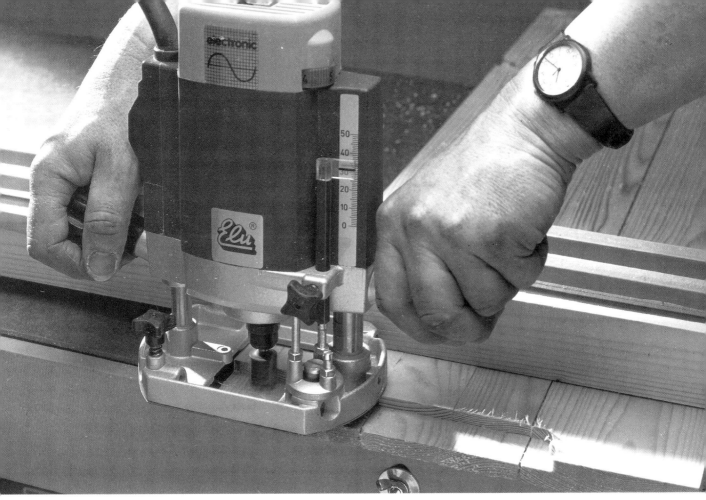

▲ FIG. 127 · ▼ FIG. 128

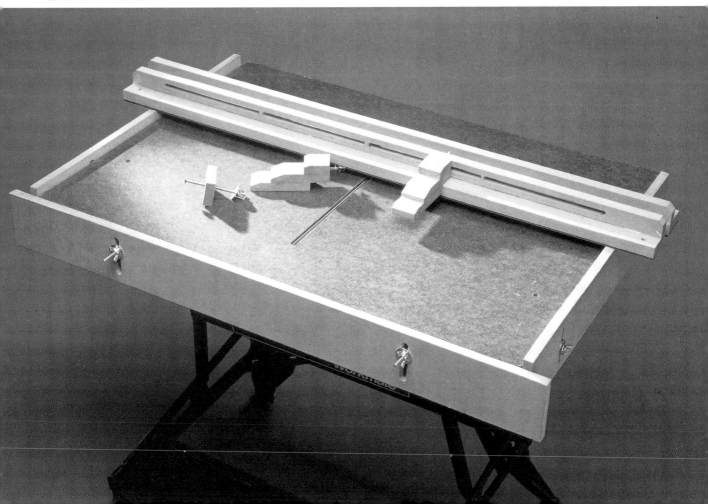

OPPOSITE ABOVE
Fig. 130 Arbor
mounted grooving
cutters can be set up to
produce a wide range of
tongue-and-groove
profiles.

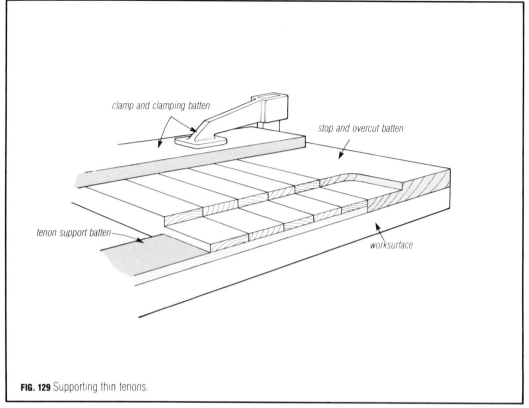

clamp and clamping batten

stop and overcut batten

tenon support batten

worksurface

FIG. 129 Supporting thin tenons.

▲ **FIG. 129**

Mortises

Mortises cut along the edge of a rail or panel can best be machined with twin side fences fitted either side of the router base. If the router is to be fed in one direction only, always use the largest-diameter cutter available, ideally equal to the width of the mortise. If, however, the mortise is to be centred by reversing the feed direction on the final cuts, a cutter of slightly smaller diameter should be used. For short deep mortises, a staggered-tooth cutter should be used as the flutes, being concentrically ground to the shank and having far less metal removed, are much stronger and less likely to whip when reaching to the full depth of the mortise. All mortises should be cut in steps of 3–6mm according to the diameter of the cutter.

Mortises can also be cut using a template to guide the path of the cutter, either clamped to the workpiece or as part of a jig. By cutting multiple templates or linking separate templates with a batten, the precise spacing of mortises can be repeated on matching or similar components.

Dowelling Joints

The precise 90° drilling facility of the plunge router can be effectively used to produce strong, accurate dowel joints, each dowel position being accurately aligned along the mating surfaces by a template or indexing strip (see page 110).

Housing Joints

The term 'housing' is generally used to describe a groove cut across the face of a board to take the squared end of a shelf or rail. Housings can easily be cut with the router using the side fence or other straight guide. Methods of using these guides for cutting single and equally spaced grooves are shown in Chapter 5.

Tongue-and-Groove Joints

Short runs of square-edged tongue-and-groove boarding can be run off successfully using a straight two-flute cutter, the depth and width of the cut set with the side fence and depth stops. The router should be set up for each rebate or groove cut along the full length of all the boards before resetting for the next operation. If a V-joint or pencil-bead edge is required, it should be cut with the appropriate cutter after the tongue or groove has been formed. However, on thin boarding it is often advisable to cut the chamfer before the groove as the thin lip may split away from the board or distort.

For longer runs, tongue-and-groove profile cutters are to be preferred, either bearing- or fence-guided. 'Off-set' cutters (Trend) of either type produce a finger joint along both edges, the board being turned over to cut the interlocking reverse profile along the second edge. While both cutters can be used in heavy-duty handheld routers, it is far safer, more accurate and easy to use them in stationary inverted or overhead machines. When setting the cutter, it should be carefully centred across the edge of the timber to ensure that the boards lie flush with one another when laid.

Tongue-and-groove profiles can be produced to specific requirements using separate grooving cutters mounted on an arbor. Using shims and spacers together with various thickness cutters, the width of each tongue or groove can be varied as required, and their depth varied by fitting cutters of different diameters. If the cutters are equally spaced a reversible joint profile can be produced similar to the off-set cutters. Alternatively, the cutters can be remounted on the arbor (or, preferably, a second arbor assembly made up) to produce the reverse profile along the opposite edge (see Fig. 130). Arbor-mounted grooving cutters can be used in both stationary or handheld routers but should be limited to cutter speeds of between 7,000 and 20,000 rpm (see page opposite). Arbor assemblies can be either fence- or bearing-guided, the latter enabling even curved edges to be jointed in this manner with ease.

Staff Bead Joints

Similar to the tongue-and-groove joint but cut with a pair of matched cutters, the staff bead joint provides a longer glue line than a butt joint in timber of equivalent thickness as well as forming a tongue or key to resist shear forces. Use staff-bead cutters to machine the concave face and a matching staff-bead jointer for the reverse profile (see Fig. 131).

▲ **FIG. 130** · ▼ **FIG. 131**

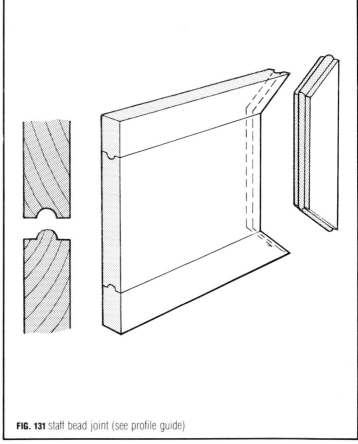

FIG. 131 staff bead joint (see profile guide)

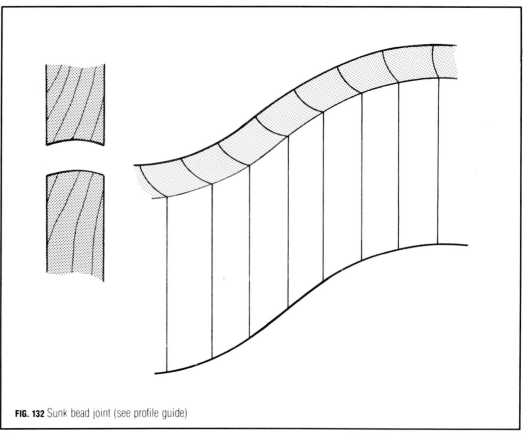

FIG. 132 Sunk bead joint (see profile guide)

▲ **FIG. 132** · ▼ **FIG. 133**

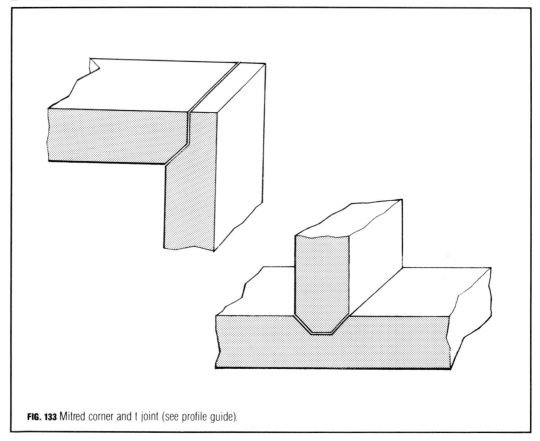

FIG. 133 Mitred corner and t joint (see profile guide).

Sunk Bead

Again cut with a matched pair of cutters but producing a curve the full thickness of the plank edge, this joint is of particular use in constructing curved structures since the curved surfaces mate closely even when the plank faces are at a slight angle to each other. For this reason it is commonly used in the building of strip-planked boat hulls and wooden tubs, since a watertight joint can be easily achieved, which eliminates the need to plane precise bevels along the plank edge. Again, the curved profile adds strength to the joint by increasing the glue line and providing some mechanical interlocking (see Fig. 132).

Mitred Joints

Flat frames or box section corners can be mitred with the router by means of a jig, a template or the sliding mitre fence on the router table (see Figs 133 and 134). Alternatively, a mitred-corner cutter set can be used, consisting of two cutters, one ground to produce a 45° stepped tongue, the other to cut a matching mitred rebate. The com-

▲ FIG. 134 · ▼ FIG. 135

ABOVE Fig. 134 When machining wide mitre faces use a three-winged surfacing cutter. These are designed with improved bottom cut characteristics for shallow surface cutting.

LEFT Fig. 135 Matched mitre corner cutters produce a strong neat lapped mitre joint. (See Profile Guide page 128.)

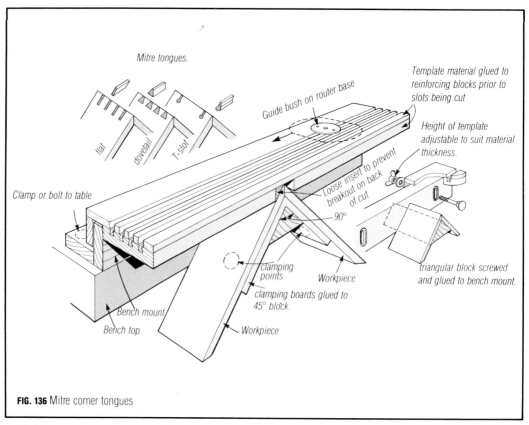

Mitre tongues.

Template material glued to
reinforcing blocks prior to
slots being cut

Guide bush on router base

Height of template
adjustable to suit material
thickness.

flat

dovetail

T-slot

Loose insert to prevent
breakout on back
of cut

90°

Clamp or bolt to table

clamping
points

Workpiece

triangular block screwed
and glued to bench mount.

clamping boards glued to
45° block.

Bench mount

Workpiece

Bench top

FIG. 136 Mitre corner tongues

▲ **FIG. 136**

bination of the two profiles produces a very strong mitre joint with adequate gluing faces (see Fig. 135).

For fastening other mitre joints various methods of positioning or angling the router can be incorporated to allow slots or holes to be accurately machined to accept loose tongues, or corner cross tongues or dowels (see Fig. 136).

Scarf Joints
Tapered scarf joints, intended for joining timber end to end or sheet materials edge to edge, can be cut with the aid of an angled jig. The length of the taper is generally given as between 8 and 10 times the thickness when joining natural timbers. Glued feather edge scarf joints used to join sheet materials need only be four times the sheet thickness. Although some woods will produce a strong glued joint at less than this, structural joints constantly under load may well need to be more. With plain-taper scarf joints the strength is reliant on the glue bond only. Keyed scarf joints are formed in the same way but are reinforced by cutting key slots

midway across the mating faces and inserting a key or, on heavy timber construction, a pair of wedges. On hooked scarf joints the mating faces are stepped to interlock, making them far stronger than the other two. For cutting scarf tapers mount the router on a wide sub-base and use a large-diameter cutter with good bottom-cut characteristics.

Finger Joints
An alternative method of joining medium-to-dense timbers end to end is to machine a series of interlocking tapered fingers into the mating faces. A single cutter is used for this purpose, mounted in an inverted or overhead stationary router. Although quick to machine, the long glue line provided by the multiple fingers produces an extremely strong neat joint (see Fig. 137).

Rule Joints
A pair of matched cutters produce the concave and convex profiles of the rule joint, traditionally used to provide a neat and attractive appearance to hinged joints on drop-leaf tables. The cutters can be used

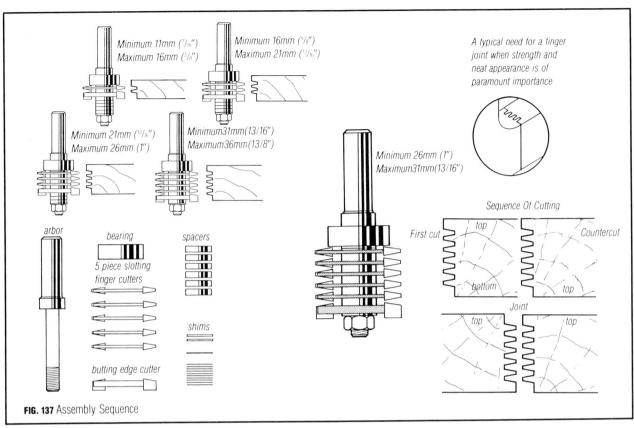

Minimum 11mm (7/16")
Maximum 16mm (5/8")

Minimum 16mm (5/8")
Maximum 21mm (13/16")

Minimum 21mm (13/16")
Maximum 26mm (1")

Minimum31mm(13/16")
Maximum36mm(13/8")

Minimum 26mm (1")
Maximum31mm(13/16")

A typical need for a finger
joint when strength and
neat appearance is of
paramount importance

arbor

bearing

spacers

5 piece slotting
finger cutters

shims

butting edge cutter

Sequence Of Cutting

First cut

top

Countercut

bottom

top

Joint

top

top

FIG. 137 Assembly Sequence

▲ FIG. 137 · ▼ FIG. 138

ABOVE Fig. 137
Finger joint cutters are
available either as a
single piece cutter or as
the more recently
introduced (Trend)
adjustable finger jointer
comprising of up to five
finger cutters and one
butting edge cutter
mounted.

LEFT Fig. 138
Matched ovolo joint
cutters can be used to
form traditional table top
hinged rule joints or
glazing bar joints.

▲ **FIG. 139**

either in the handheld router guided with the side fence or in inverted or overhead stationary machines (see Fig. 138).

Scribed Joints
Another useful router-cut joint can be formed using a profile/scribing cutter or cutter set (see pages 162 and 163). Designed initially to cut the panel groove and edge moulding and to scribe the reverse moulding on the rail ends when assembling framed panels. The tongue produced by the reverse profile, when glued into the panel rebate, forms an extremely strong joint. This method eliminates the need to cut separate corner joints and is adequate for most cabinet-door and light panel-framing situations (see Fig. 139).

Dovetails and Dovetail Housings
When cutting the tongue to fit into a dovetail housing it is important that both sides are cut evenly and parallel to each other. This is best achieved by clamping the board between a pair of angled guides either fitted to the edge of the work bench or held in the vice jaws. The guides are formed from battens glued to equal-width parallel boards to form a precise right angle. In use the boards are clamped to provide a flush surface over which the router can slide, the outer edges acting as guide faces for the router's side fence. Set the cutter to cut to the full depth of the dovetail tongue in one pass and the side fence to position the cut in from the face of the board. Feed the router from each end, the side fence running against opposite edges in turn (see Fig. 140).

The housing can be cut across the face of the workpiece using a single or parallel straight edge to guide the base of the router and cutting to the full depth of the dovetail housing in one pass (see Fig. 141).

Dovetail Jigs
The versatile Leigh dovetail jig can be used to cut most traditional types of dovetail, including through, half-blind, sliding and end-to-end. Unlike most dovetail jigs, and machines the pitch and spacing of each pin and socket can be varied which enables unequally spaced dovetails of any size to be produced in timber up to 32mm thick. The

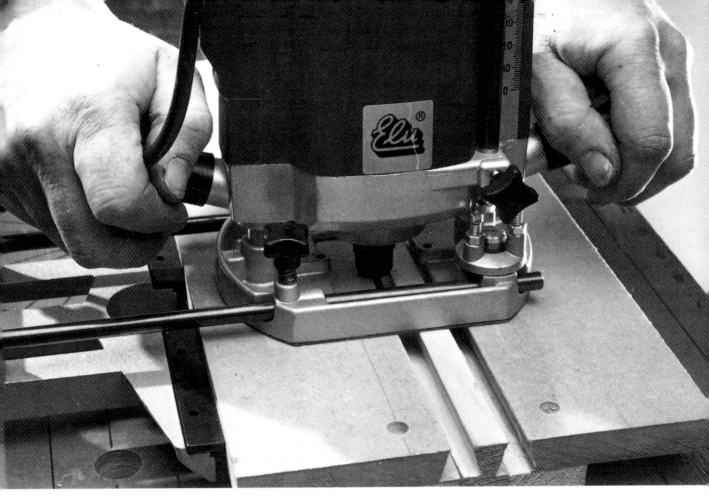

versatility of the Leigh dovetailer results from the patented adjustable template designed to allow simultaneous setting of both the pins and sockets to ensure a precise fit.

The precision of the finished dovetails is ensured by the micro-screw adjustment for setting the required cutter diameter and the ease of setting the separate fingers against a rule or spacing gauge. Fine setting for depth of cut is carried out with a fine vertical adjuster fitted to the router. By fitting a single or individual bridges between the ends of the straight fingers, the jig can be used for cutting sliding dovetail housings, rebates, grooves and short tenons. For cutting mortise-and-tenon joints of variable carcass length on the Leigh jig, an optional attachment which replaces the finger template is available (see Figs 142 and 143).

ELU Dovetail Jig
The ELU jig is designed for cutting 13·5mm-long through or lap dovetails in timber between 12mm and 30mm thick and up to 300mm wide (see Figs 144 and 145). With the jig secured to the edge of a workbench,

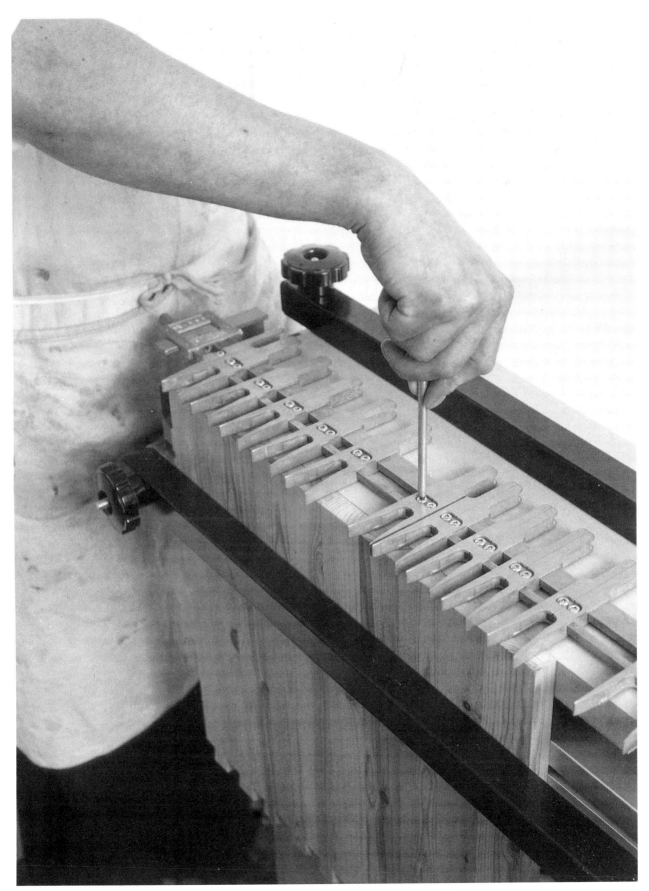

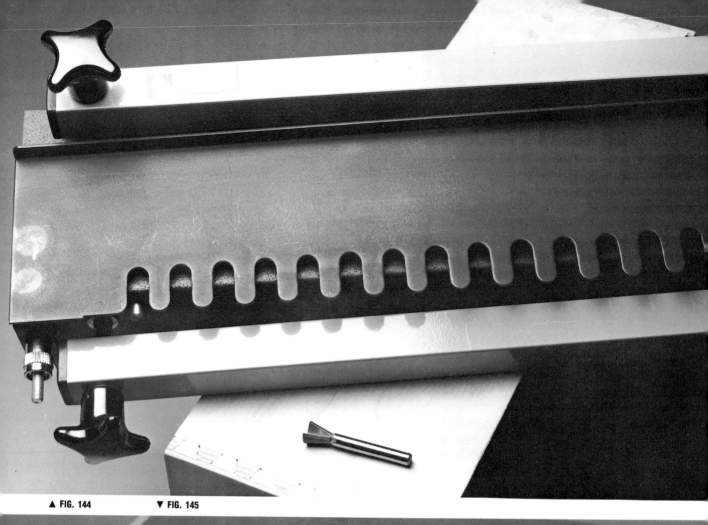

▲ FIG. 144   ▼ FIG. 145

▲ **FIG. 146**

the two pieces of timber are held by clamping bars at 90° to each other with a straight fingered template mounted over the mating edges. A guide bush is fitted to the base of the router and a dovetail cutter fitted in the collet, the depth of cut being set by the depth gauge supplied with the jig. To achieve precise settings the optional fine depth adjuster should be fitted to ELU routers. Once set up the router is simply slid over the face of the template, the guide bush engaging between each pair of fingers. In this way both the pins and the sockets are cut in one operation, alignment stops on the jig having offset the mating faces so that the edges line up when the joint is assembled. Although most makes of router can be used with the ELU dovetail jig those (other than the ELU 96 and 96E) having one or both base dimensions less than 150mm should be fitted with a wider sub-base or adaptor plate (adaptor plates are available from Trend).

Keller Dovetail Templates

Made from thick aluminium plate, the templates are supplied in pairs along with the appropriate cutters, one straight-fingered together with a dovetail cutter for cutting the sockets, the other angled with a straight cutter for the pins. Both cutters have shank-mounted guide bearings. In use, each template is screwed to a squared batten which can be clamped to the timber being joined. The sockets are cut first after carefully positioning the template from one end of the workpiece. From this the socket positions are then scribed onto the second piece and the pin template aligned and clamped to it, slotted screw holes in the template allowing for slight adjustment in the length of the pins (see Fig. 146). Three template lengths are available to suit boards approximately 400mm, 600mm, and 900mm wide, and from 4·5mm to 16mm, 9mm to 25mm, and 16mm to 32mm thick respectively. The distance between the pins is larger for each length (28·5mm, 44·5mm and 76mm respectively). However, if the template is moved along the workpiece and the last and first dovetail positions carefully centred, each template can be used on any width of board.

12 | Maintenance

To consistently achieve neat, accurate results safely, as with all power and hand tools, both routers and cutters must be carefully maintained with regular checks and servicing. While any major servicing, repairs or cutter regrinding should be left to an experienced service engineer, many of the checks and light maintenance should be carried out by the operator as routine prior to the machine being used. During use any unusual variation in the sound or any vibration should be investigated immediately.

Routers

Until underload, the centrifugal effect of the high-speed router makes it appear to run smoothly, and it is often not until the cutter enters the work that any slight misalignment, wear or other fault becomes obvious, possibly with ruinous results. It is therefore imperative that the machine is regularly cleaned and checked to make apparent and give adequate warning of any possible problems that might arise.

In manufacture electric routers are assembled with a high degree of precision to ensure that they can sustain these high working speeds and maintain a high standard of performance over a reasonable length of service. Any adverse treatment or lack of general maintenance will seriously impair that performance, as can repair or major servicing or unnecessary dismantling by anyone other than an authorized (if under guarantee) and experienced service engineer.

Routine maintenance should include re-moval of dust, swarf and chips, preferably by blowing through with compressed air or a powerful vacuum, and wiping over with a soft cloth using a mild solvent to remove resin, glue, oils or grease deposits. The plunge columns should be lightly lubricated, preferably with an oil- and wax-free lubri-cant such as the dry PTFE-based type (see Fig. 147). These lubricants avoid the risk of leaving oil or wax traces to either mar the surface of the work or affect surface finishes applied over them. Take particular care to remove deposits from the underside of the base which may prevent it from sliding smoothly over the surface of the work. Also check the base for scratches or nicks, which could have a similar effect or mar the surface of the work. Remove any burrs gently with very fine wirewool or wet and dry abrasive paper. Check that all side fence rods slide easily and that clamping screws tighten fully without pitting the surface of the rods. Remove any burrs from the end of the screws or the rod surface gently with fine wet and dry abrasive. Fence rods generally slide easily without the use of a lubricant, but if necessary again use a dry PTFE-based one. Check all other locking screws and ensure that antivibration springs are fitted where originally fitted. Carefully clean the threads of the collet lock nut and inspect it for any damage that might lead to binding. Any problem should be referred to a service engineer. Do not try recutting threads with a file or other means as any misalignment will cause damage to the cutter shank and an imbalance in operations.

Many switch faults are caused by dust deposits on the contacts, which can often be removed by sucking out with a vacuum cleaner. However, switch faults are best solved by having the complete switch replaced, which avoids much recurring annoyance.

To check for wear, remove the collet and lock nut from the shaft and feel for anything other than absolute minimal end play in the shaft. Spin the shaft and feel for any grating, side play or unevenness in the bearings or shaft seating in the bearings. If there is any suggestion of play or any doubt, have the router checked by the manufacturer's approved service engineers. Replace the collet and lock nut and insert any cutter with a perfect unworn shank. Tighten the collet to the first stop by hand and check for any obvious side movement. Another indication of a worn or faulty collet is brown rust-like markings left on the cutter shank after use. If in doubt, have the collet checked and replace it if necessary. Carry out this check for each size of collet used with a specific machine.

Regularly check the condition of the power lead for chafed insulation, kinks or broken conductors. If supplied with a continental plug, avoid adaptors and replace the plug with one suited to the power source socket it is connected to. Ensure that all fuses are correctly rated. For all portable routers on 220 to 240 volts, fit a 13-amp fuse, for 110 to 115 volt machines up to 1,500 watts, a 15-amp fuse; for over 1,500 watts, a 20-amp fuse. As a general guide for extension cables, never use a cable rated less than the original power lead fitted to the router.

Motor brushes should not be allowed to wear down to a point where they are causing excess sparking or intermittent running. This will result quickly in irreparable damage to the commutator. As they are generally inexpensive and readily available, always replace brushes rather than attempt to clean them up.

Simply listening to any variation in the noise a router produces and noting the presence of any vibration is a good guide to how well it is functioning.

Cutters

To maintain the balance between cutter durability and quality of finish, cutters must

▲ **FIG. 147**

not only be kept sharp but retain their original cutting and clearance angles throughout their serviceable life.

One important aspect of cutter design and manufacture is that of balance. The centrifugal force of a high-speed cutter is extremely high and any imbalance will cause vibration between the cutter and workpiece, resulting in an inferior finish and possible damage to the router bearings. All large-diameter high-speed router cutters have two or more cutting edges, each perfectly matched to the others during manufacture to ensure perfect balance. The same applies to all other smaller cutters with two or more cutting edges. This balance must be maintained if or when it becomes necessary to regrind a cutter. Also, any difference in the size or profile of each flute could virtually halve the cutting speed and effectiveness of the cutter since only one or one and a part of the flutes would be doing most of the work.

It is therefore essential to have cutters reground professionally, where it can be done on highly sophisticated equipment which will reproduce the original cutter geometry perfectly. Bearing in mind the

ABOVE Fig. 147 The plunge columns should be regularly cleaned and lightly lubricated with a light machine oil or perferably a wax and grease free spray lubricant. PTFE lubricant can be used if sprayed as a very light film.

RIGHT Fig. 148 TCT and solid carbide cutters can be sharpened on the inside face by honing on a diamond-slurry-impregnated abrasive tile, taking care not to damage the tips or guide pins (remove bearings).

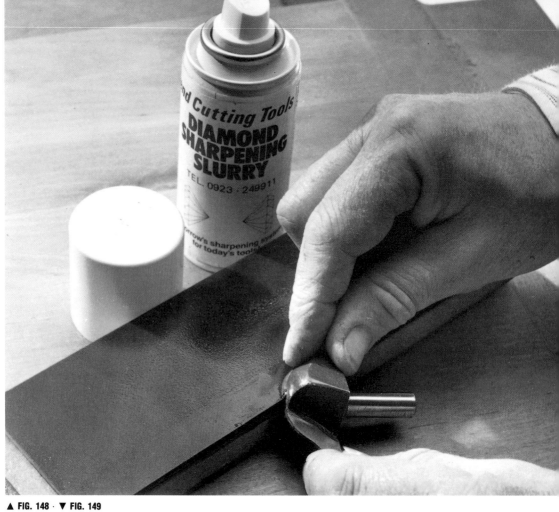

▲ FIG. 148 · ▼ FIG. 149

RIGHT Fig. 149 HSE and HSSE cutters can be honed on the flat inside face on a fine flat oilstone using a little light machine oil taking care not to damage the tips, or guide pins (remove bearings).

initial cost of cutters and the surprisingly low cost of having them professionally reground, it is certainly not worth the risk of ruining them by doing it yourself.

Until recently it was common practice when regrinding cutters to use abrasive wheels of standard or white aluminium oxide for high-speed steel (HSS) cutters (they produce the best results but wear quicker) and wheels of green grit for rough-cutting solid and tipped tungsten carbide cutters (SC and TCT), followed by lapping on a diamond wheel. However, leading professional companies such as Trend, recommend that special diamond wheels fitted to precision grinding machinery should be used throughout the grinding process. The reason for this is that not only do diamond wheels produce a superior finish but they retain their edges far longer, an important factor in maintaining a constant profile.

Being relatively expensive, diamond wheels are not generally available or cost-effective for amateur or small professional workshop use.

All cutters can, however, be kept sharp by regular honing until such time as the cutting edges start to round over or damage is sustained. On high-speed steel (HSS and HSSE) cutters this can be carried out on a flat oilstone. Although solid or tipped tungsten cutters can be honed to some extent on an oilstone it is far more effective to use a diamond-slurry-impregnated tile as supplied by Trend. The diamond slurry is supplied in aerosols in three grades of medium, fine and superfine. These can be used for all metals and metal compounds, including HSS and TCT. Medium grade (Trend ref., DMK/M red) is used for rapid sharpening and the removal of grinding marks from router and other machine cutters, and all other cutting tools; fine, to leave a superior finish on the cutting edge of tools of all kinds; superfine (DMK/SF white), to produce a particularly keen edge on chisels, plane irons, and carving and other fine cutting tools. The slurry is initially applied to the surface of a specially prepared tile (supplied as a kit with the slurry). Lay the cutter on the tile with the face flat on the surface and, using light finger pressure only, rub to and fro along the face of the tile (see Fig. 148).

Honing – first on a medium abrasive stone or slurry, finishing with fine – is always carried out along the inside or leading face of a cutter. This is generally a flat face which can be laid flat on the surface of the oilstone or slurry tile (see Fig. 149). Only the slightest amount of metal should be removed, normally not even enough to raise a burr or HSS cutters, but if a burr is left along the cutting edge remove it very lightly on a rubberised slipstone or leather pad.

Sharpening on oilstones should be carried out in a similar way, using a thin oil as a cutting agent. The inside face of curved flutes, such as on some single-flute cutters, can be lightly honed with a fine round-edge slipstone.

If regular sharpening and honing has not been carried out and the cutter is very blunt but not damaged, it should be sent to a specialist servicing company to be professionally resharpened.

It is well worth getting into the habit of taking the cutter out of the collet immediately the operation or series of operations is complete and quickly checking it before putting it away. Any resin or other deposits that won't simply blow off can generally be removed with lighter fuel or other solvent. The bearings of self-guiding cutters, in particular those used for trimming laminates, often get gummed up with adhesive or resin. Regularly remove the bearing and scrape off any adhesive to prevent it building up. If the bearing is cleaned with an adhesive solvent the bearing grease will be dissolved and is difficult to replace on all but the larger-diameter bearings. If you do manage to regrease make sure to clean any traces of grease from the external parts of the bearing to avoid marring future work. The heat created by the cutter will soften contact and some other types of adhesive. To minimize this effect remove excess adhesive after assembling the workpiece and allow the adhesive to harden fully before trimming. Clean fixed-pin guides with a solvent and check the pin for ovality or burrs.

> ⚠️ **Safety Tip**
>
> Take care not to cut yourself on the cutting edges. For safety wear a thin leather gardening glove or use a wooden holder to grip the cutter. Do not rub your hands together after using diamond slurry but wash to remove any residue.

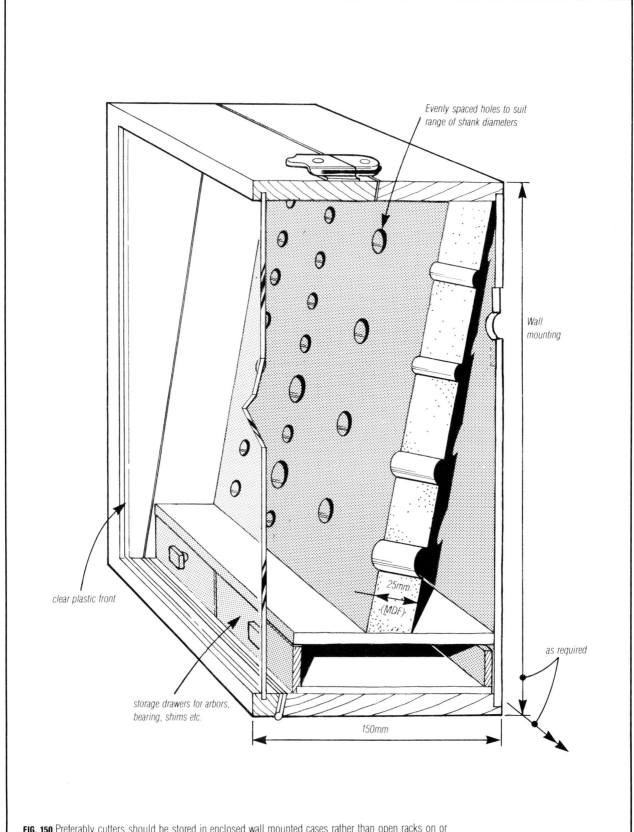

Evenly spaced holes to suit
range of shank diameters

Wall
mounting

clear plastic front

25mm.

·(MDF).

as required

storage drawers for arbors,
bearing, shims etc.

150mm

FIG. 150 Preferably cutters should be stored in enclosed wall mounted cases rather than open racks on or
close to the worksurface or bench, and should be returned immediately they are withdrawn from the collet.

Cutter Storage

Cutters should never be put loose into a box with others. Always put them into separate compartments or into a rack drilled to take the shanks. When carrying them keep them separate in a padded case. Never store cutters in damp conditions as they will rust quickly, which causes surface pitting and cutting-edge fatigue. If damp conditions are unavoidable, spray cutters with light oil before storing them, but clean it off before use to avoid marring the surface of the work (see Fig. 150).

Common Causes of Router Cutter Failure

1 Broken Cutters

Most common with small diameter cutters, where feed pressure is too great or the depth of cut in a single pass is too deep. Always allow the router to attain full rpm before feeding the cutter into the work.

2 Chipped Carbide

This usually indicates that the operator has hit a hard obstruction embedded in the work, such as a nail or stone. Alternatively, lack of attention has caused the operator to hit a cramp, vice jaw or other obstruction with the protruding part of the cutter beneath the work. Chips or flakes can also break from the cutting edge if it has been reground too often, leaving it thin and fragile.

3 Damaged Guide Bearing

Bearings nearly always fail because the grease has been dissolved during cleaning. If there is any doubt as to the condition of the bearing, replace it.

4 Faulty Brazing

Poor brazing can be identified by gaps or voids in a brazed seam, which may leave it weak. This can lead to the tip separating from the cutter. As this is a manufacturing fault and can be reasonably easily proved to be the cause, it will be covered under any reputable manufacturer's warranty.

5 Burning

This generally indicates too slow a feed rate, too deep a cut, or that the cutter requires resharpening or regrinding before use.

6 Fretting Corrosion

This shows up as brown rust-like markings on the shank. It is generally caused by a worn or overtightened collet. Fretting will cause excessive vibration and sudden cutter failure. Cutters showing these marks are unlikely to be replaced under any warranty. At the slightest indication of fretting the collet must be checked and, if necessary, replaced.

◄ **FIG. 150**

The cutters featured in this profile
guide are the products and copyright
of Trend Machinery and Cutting
Tools Ltd. They are widely available
through a network of stockists
throughout Great Britain, but if you
have difficulty in obtaining them, you
should contact:

Trend Machinery and Cutting
Tools Ltd
Unit N, Penfold Works
Imperial Way
Watford WD2 4YF
Hertfordshire
England

Telephone: (0923) 249911
Fax: (0923) 36879

13 | Profile Guide

Although the comprehensive range of router cutters now available caters for a wide range of jointing and decorative machining operations, as when using other shaping and moulding machines, it is also possible to produce far more complex shapes and sections by using a combination of these standard cutter profiles. This is of particular use to the designer and/or craftsman in the production of special sections, for example in the construction of high performance joinery to ensure good weathering and draught-proofing characteristics. A combination of cutter profiles can also be used to create new, or match existing, decorative profiles and mouldings in the design of modern or reproduction furniture as well as in joinery and restoration work.

However, finding the right cutter, or an alternative, when one or other is not available is not always straightforward and is, at the least, time-consuming.

To simplify the task, the following Profile Guide is designed to give quick, clear reference to approximately 1,000 profile variations. It includes those produced using the standard range of router cutter, possible variations on them using different diameter pilot guides, as well as cutter depth and fence settings. The guide also shows how to produce complex profiles using a combination of various standard cutter profiles. For clarity and ease of identification, profiles of a similar shape are grouped together under their descriptive heading, along with an illustration of the relative standard cutter. To accommodate the full range of cutters, cutters of the same shape but available in a range of sizes are illustrated by only one sample cutter but with the profile sections formed using each size.

Each cutter illustration and profile section is drawn full size to allow the user to trace off relative cutter shapes when composing new or matching existing profiles. However, care should be taken to allow for any slight variations in the reproduced size which may occur during the printing of this book. Ideally, lined tracing paper should be used for this purpose, the moulding or section being drawn or traced onto the paper. The shape can then be analysed to divide it into its various elements: ogee, ovolo, chamfer, bead, rebate etc, and each element identified from the relative section in the profile guide. From this, the cutter illustration can be matched to the cutter manufacturers reference. Where appropriate, key dimensions such as those relating to corner and bearing radii (example R 9·5 = Radius 9·5 millimetres), are shown in millimetres with a conversion chart to imperial equivalents.

Composite shapes can be produced using either handheld or stationary routing machines. However, the sequence of operations must be carefully planned to allow each cut and pass to be safely made in the most efficient order so that the maximum amount of flat surface bears against the machine guide or fence for each subsequent cut. In many cases, these problems can be reduced by cutting the composite shape from oversize material, allowing adequate waste to act as guide surfaces and facilitate clamping. Alternatively, introduce temporary guide surfaces held with double-sided tape or clamps. When it is necessary to remove large amounts of waste material, straight or rebate cutters can be employed to reduce the work load on the more complex, and less efficient, decorative profile cutters.

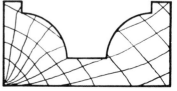

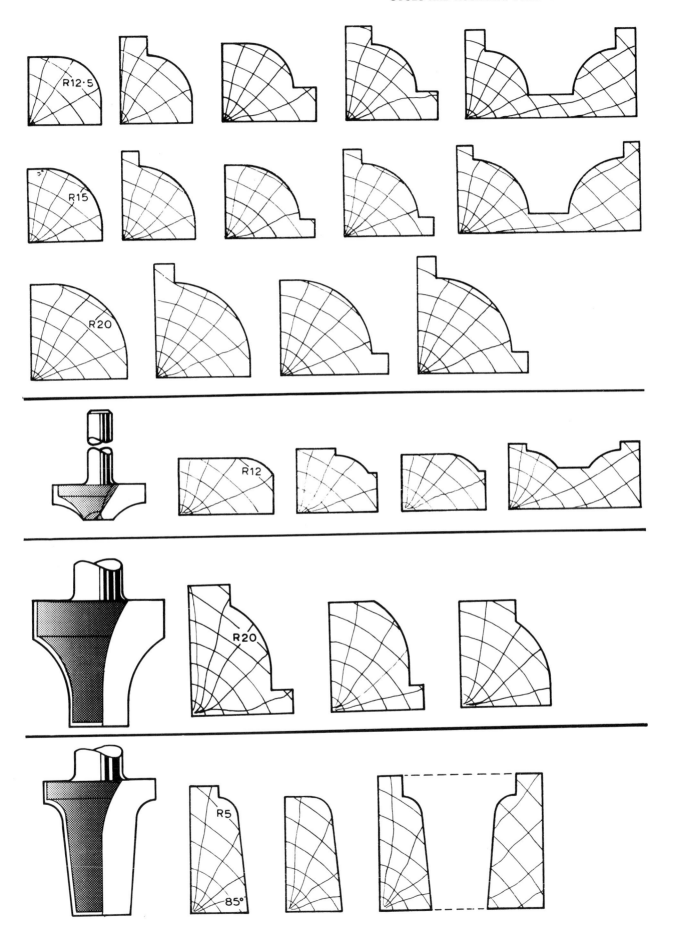

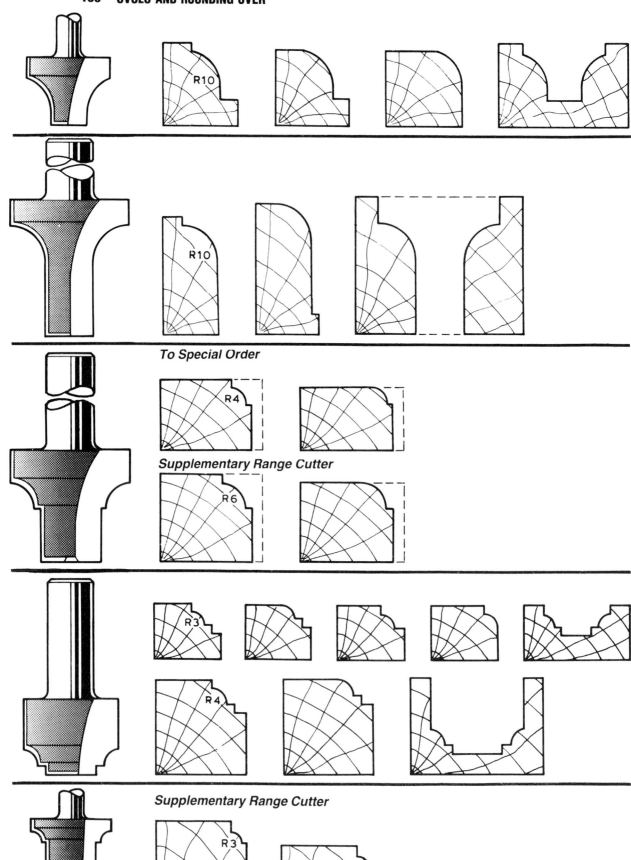

To Special Order

Supplementary Range Cutter

Supplementary Range Cutter

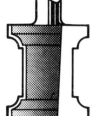

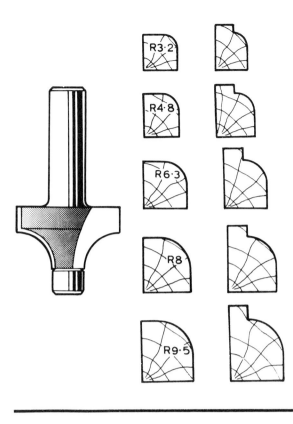

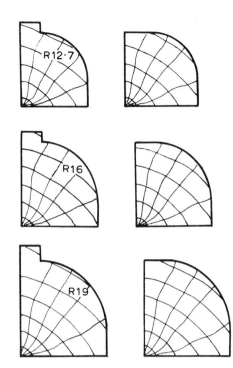

R3·2
R4·8
R6·3
R8
R9·5

R12·7
R16
R19

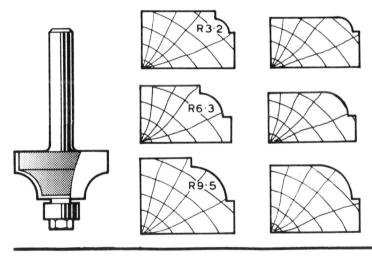

R3·2
R6·3
R9·5

with 9.5mm bearing

with 9.5mm bearing

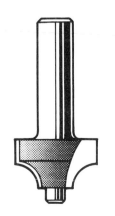

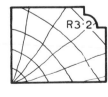
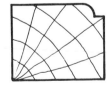

R3·2

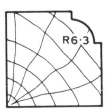
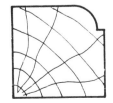

R6·3

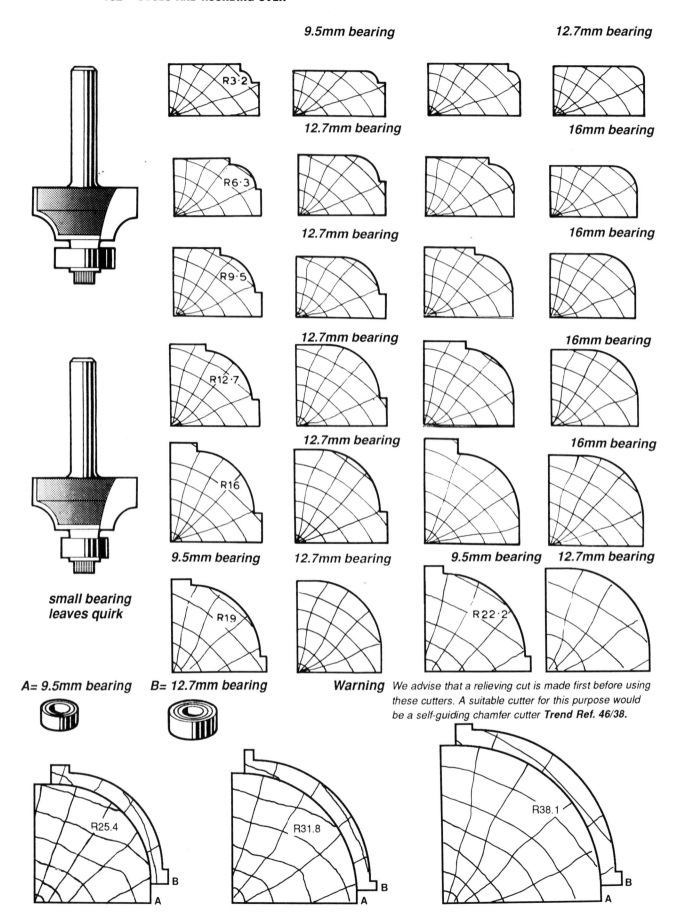

9.5mm bearing

12.7mm bearing

R3·2

12.7mm bearing

16mm bearing

R6·3

12.7mm bearing

16mm bearing

R9·5

12.7mm bearing

16mm bearing

R12·7

12.7mm bearing

16mm bearing

R16

9.5mm bearing

12.7mm bearing

9.5mm bearing

12.7mm bearing

R19

R22·2

small bearing
leaves quirk

A= 9.5mm bearing

B= 12.7mm bearing

Warning We advise that a relieving cut is made first before using
these cutters. A suitable cutter for this purpose would
be a self-guiding chamfer cutter **Trend Ref. 46/38.**

R25.4

R31.8

R38.1

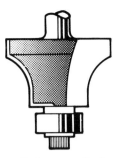

  12.7mm bearing *16mm bearing*

Only supplied with 12.7mm bearing

 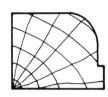 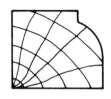 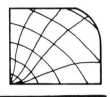

12.7mm bearing   *16mm bearing*

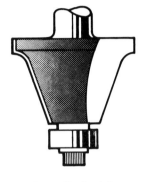

Supplied with both bearings

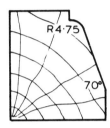 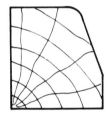 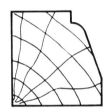 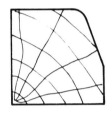

12.7mm bearing   *16mm bearing*

9.5mm bearing   *12.7mm bearing*

Supplied with both bearings

   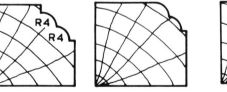 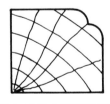

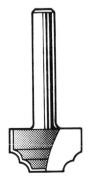

   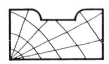 

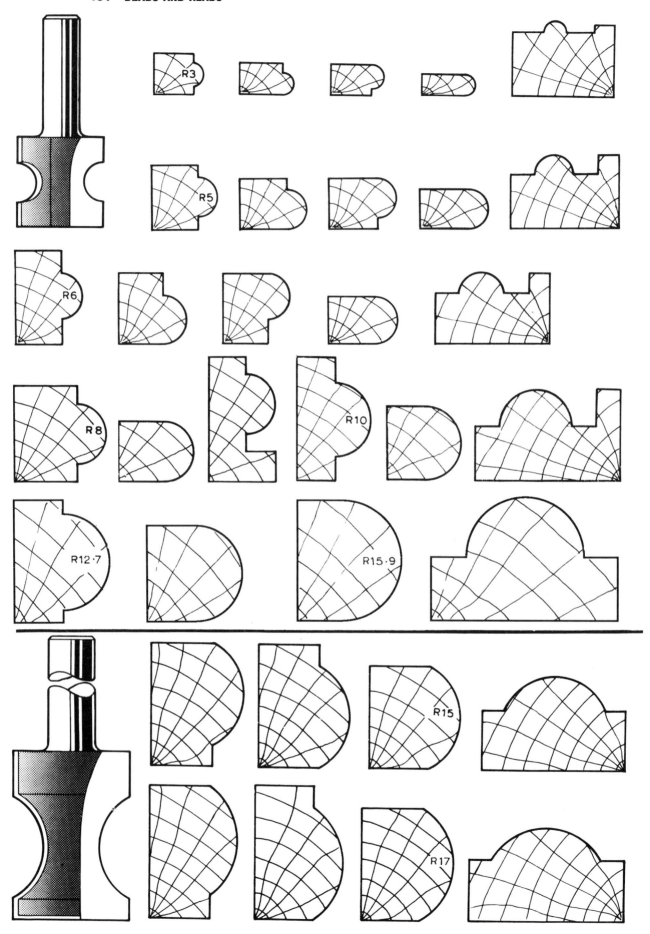

R3

R5

R6

R8

R10

R12·7

R15·9

R15

R17

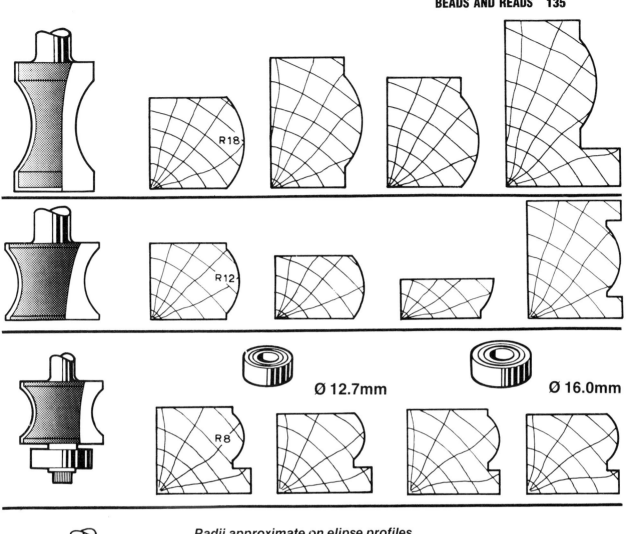

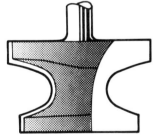

Ø 12.7mm   Ø 16.0mm

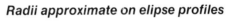

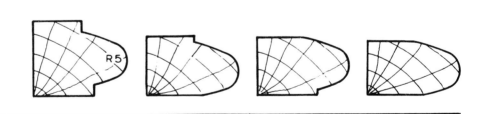

Radii approximate on elipse profiles

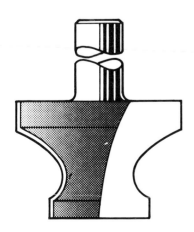

Radii approximate on elipse profiles

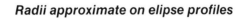

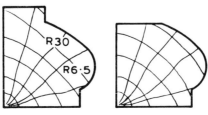

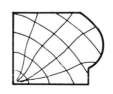

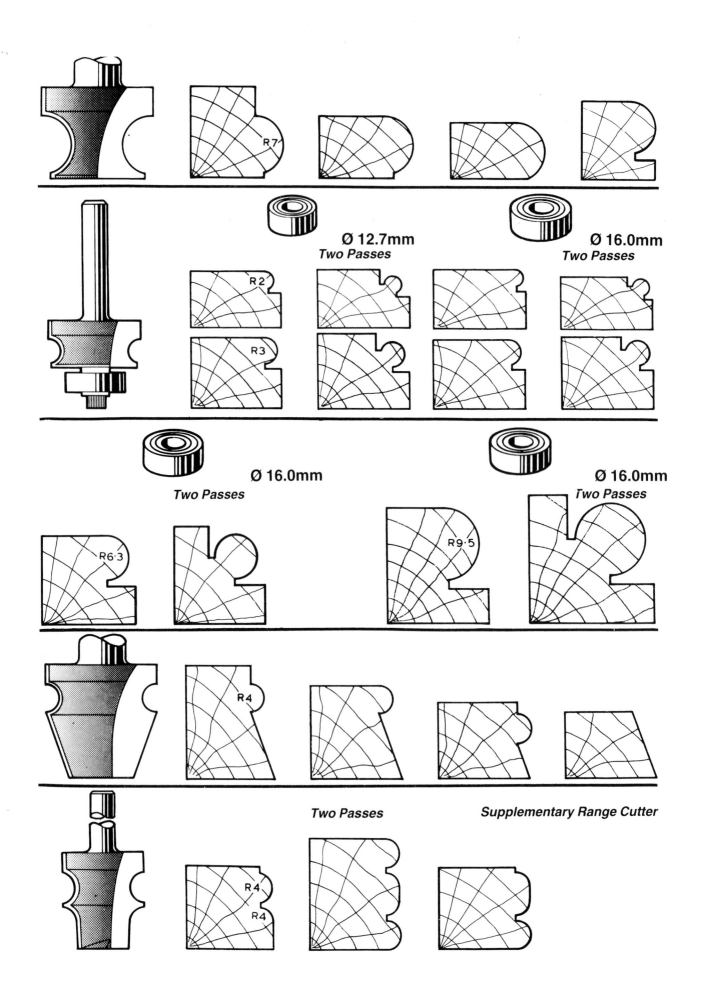

R 7

Ø 12.7mm
Two Passes

Ø 16.0mm
Two Passes

R 2

R 3

Ø 16.0mm

Two Passes

Ø 16.0mm
Two Passes

R6·3

R9·5

R 4

Two Passes

Supplementary Range Cutter

R 4
R 4

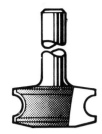

Supplementary Range Cutter

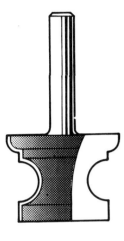

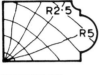
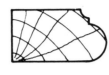
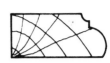

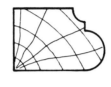
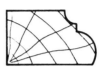

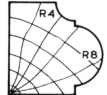
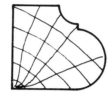
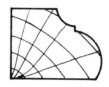

*Supplementary
Range Cutter*

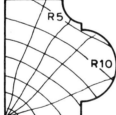
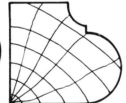
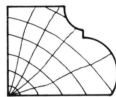
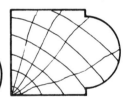

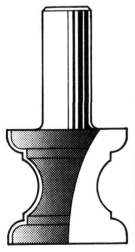

*Supplementary
Range Cutter*

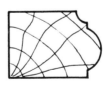
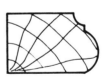

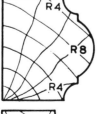
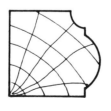
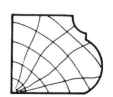
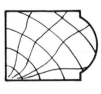

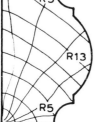
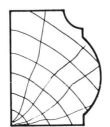
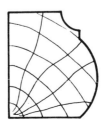
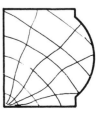

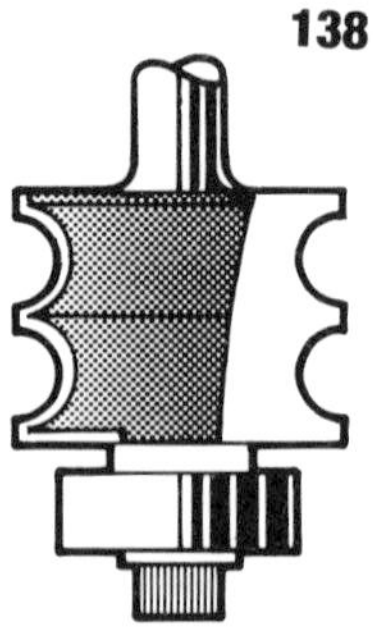

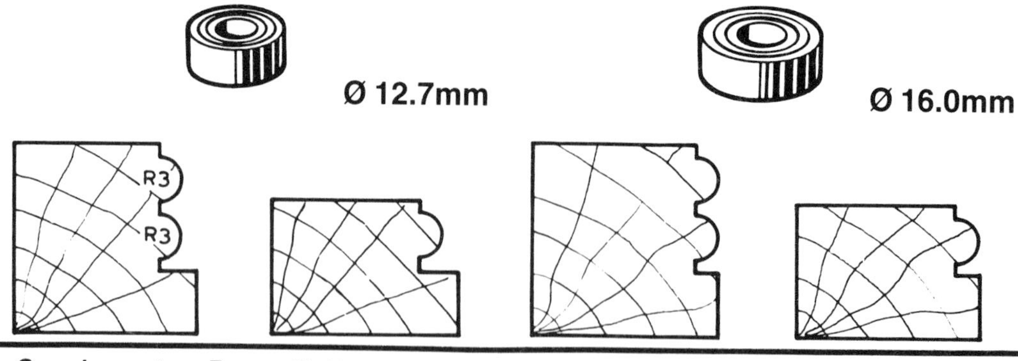

Ø 12.7mm

Ø 16.0mm

*Only supplied
with 16mm
bearing*

R3
R3

Supplementary Range Cutter

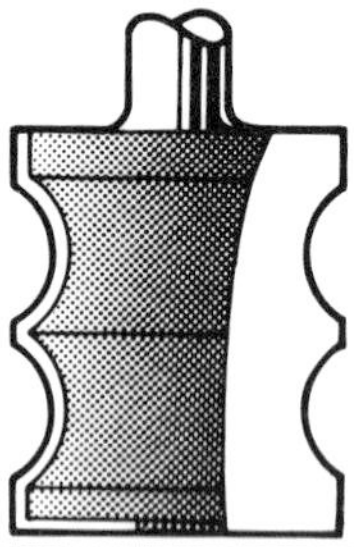

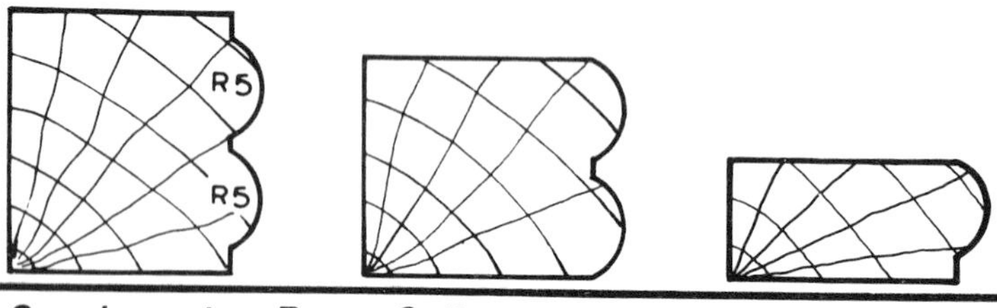

R5
R5

Supplementary Range Cutter

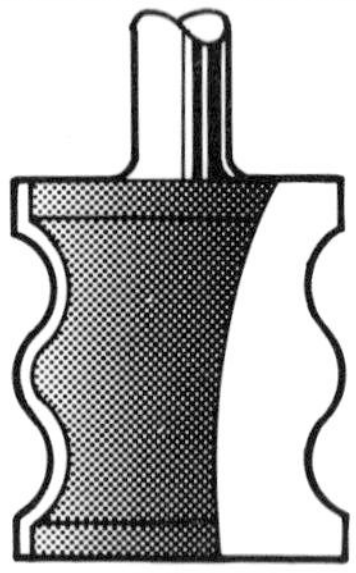

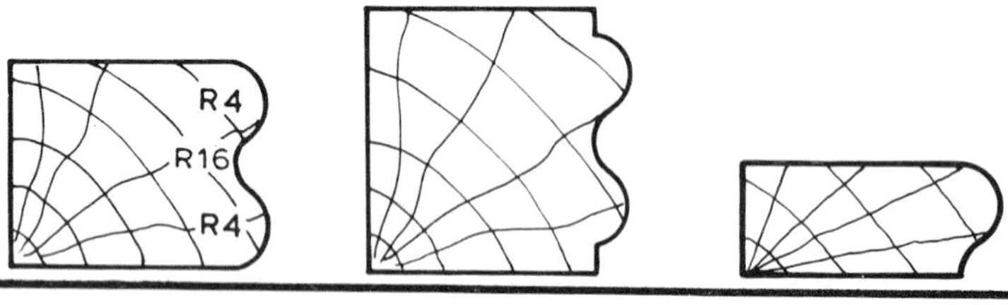

R4
R16
R4

Supplementary Range Cutter

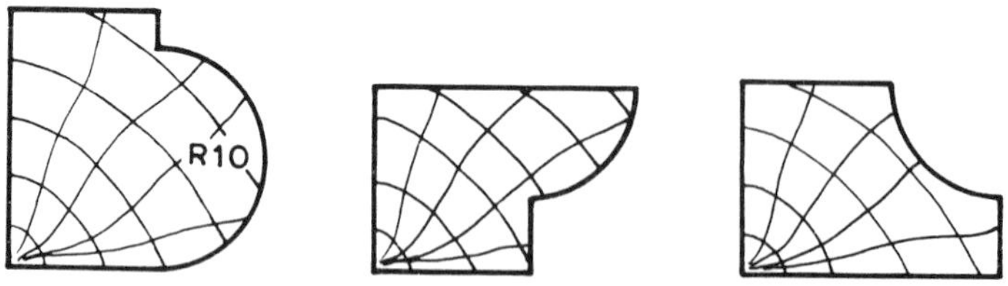

R10

Supplementary Range Cutter

R9
R9

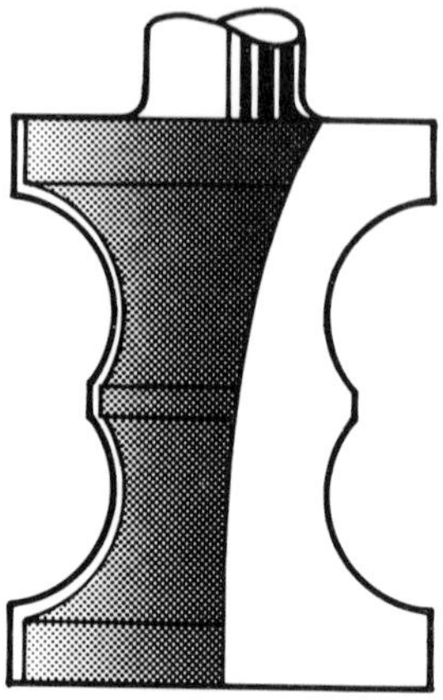

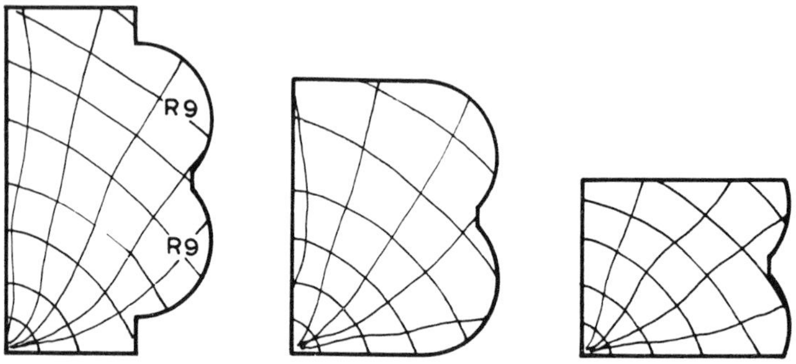

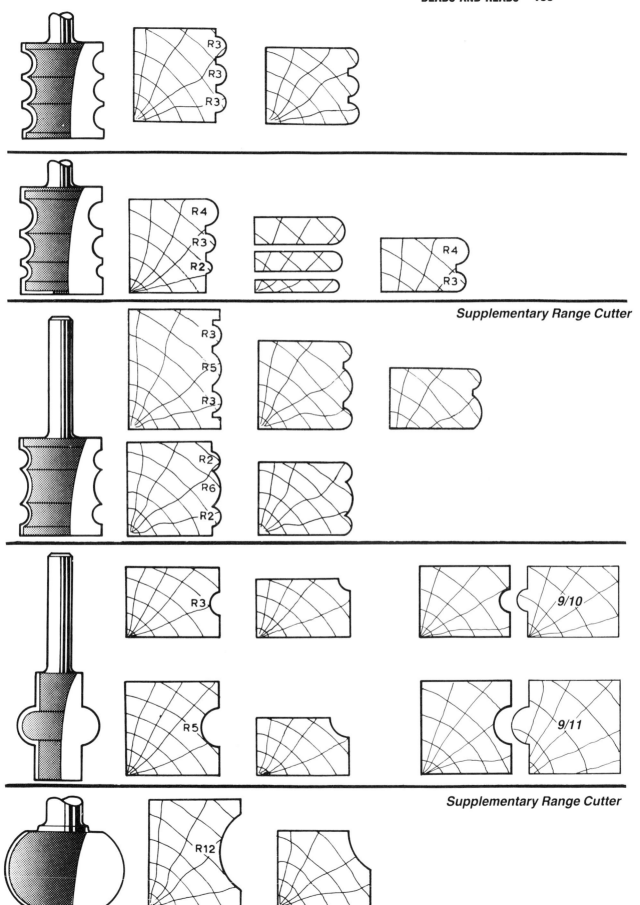

Supplementary Range Cutter

Supplementary Range Cutter

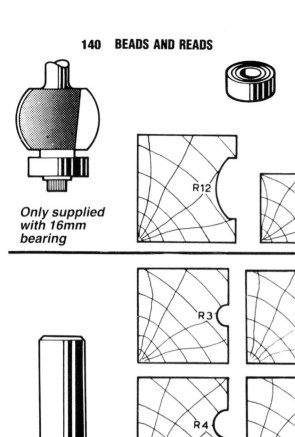

*Only supplied
with 16mm
bearing*

Ø 12.7mm

Ø 16.0mm

*Supplementary
Range Cutter*

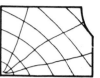

Supplementary Range Cutter

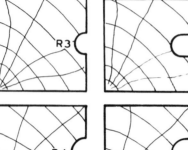

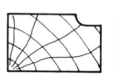

Supplementary Range Cutter

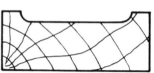

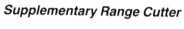

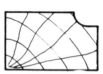

Supplementary Range Cutter

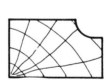

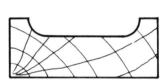

Supplementary Range Cutter

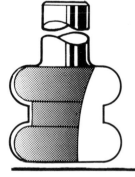

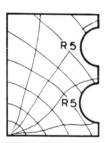

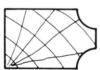

Ø 12.7mm

Ø 16.0mm

*Supplementary
Range Cutter*

*Only supplied
with 16mm
bearing*

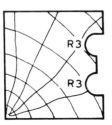

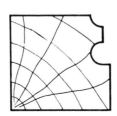

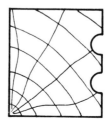

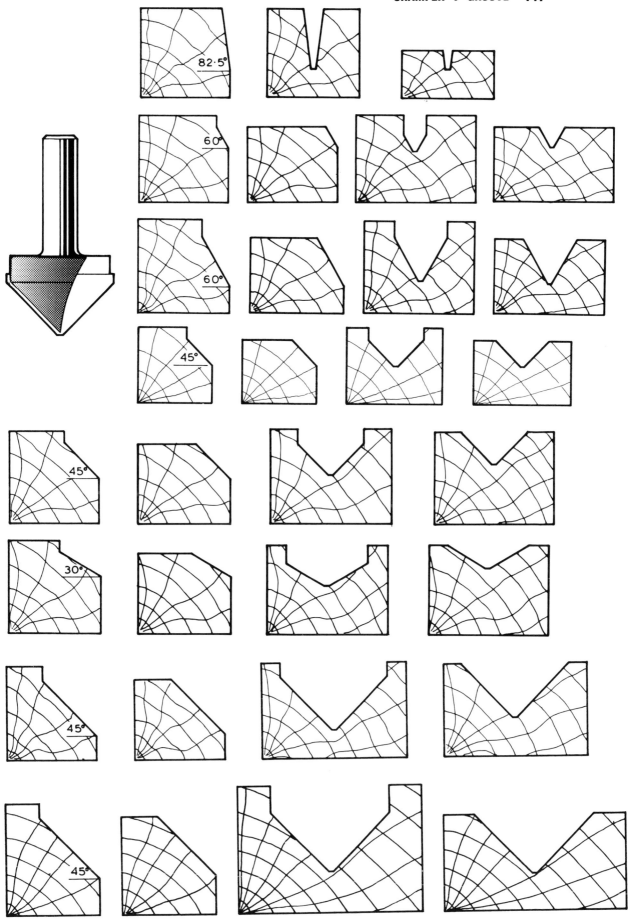

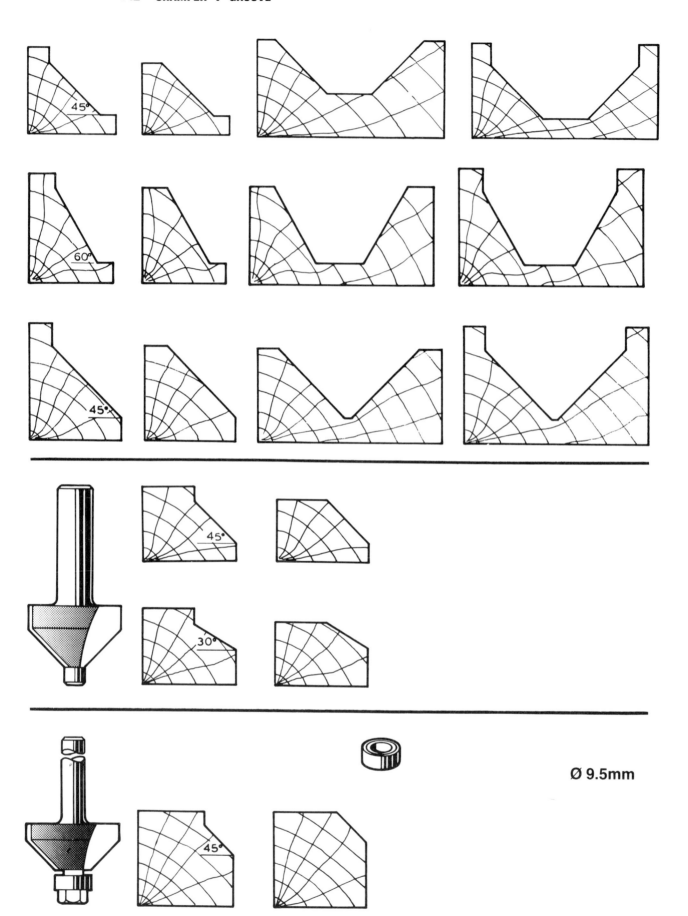

Ø 9.5mm

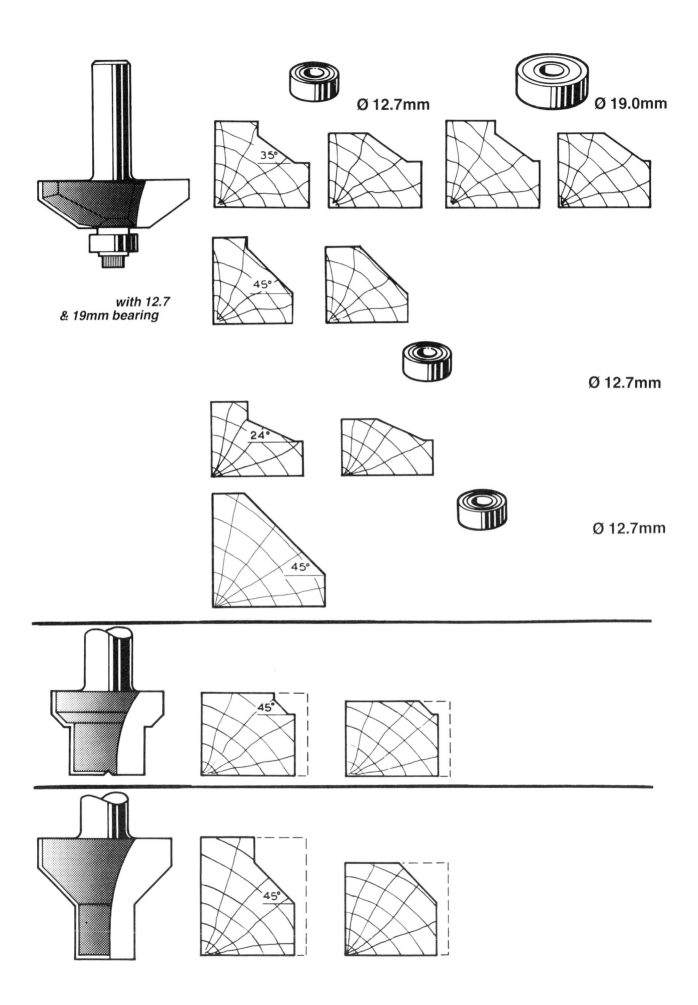

Ø 12.7mm

Ø 19.0mm

with 12.7
& 19mm bearing

35°

45°

Ø 12.7mm

24°

Ø 12.7mm

45°

45°

45°

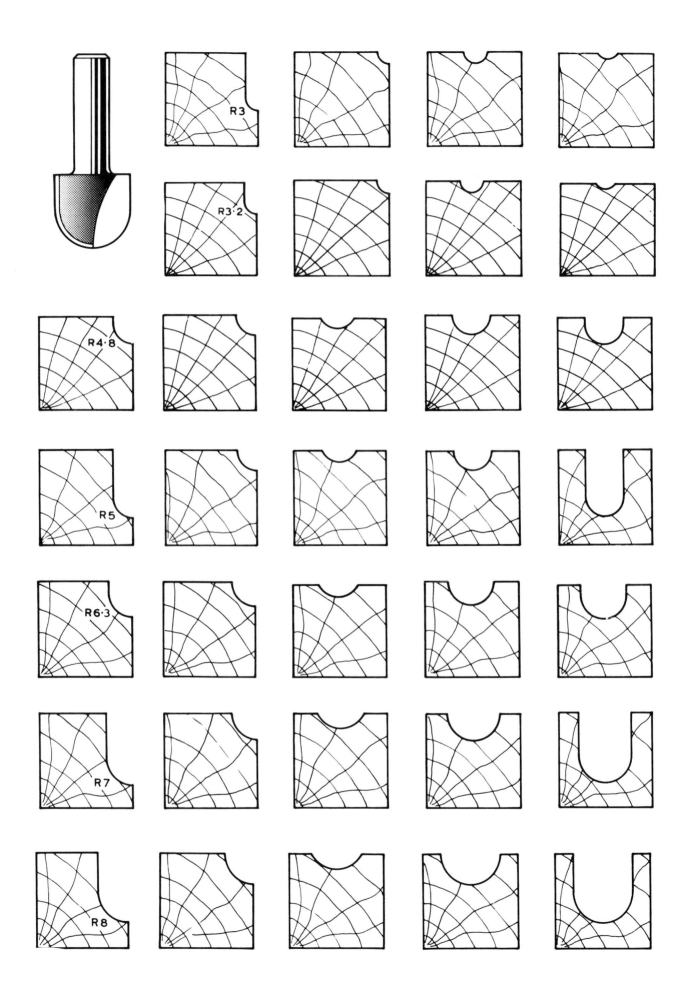

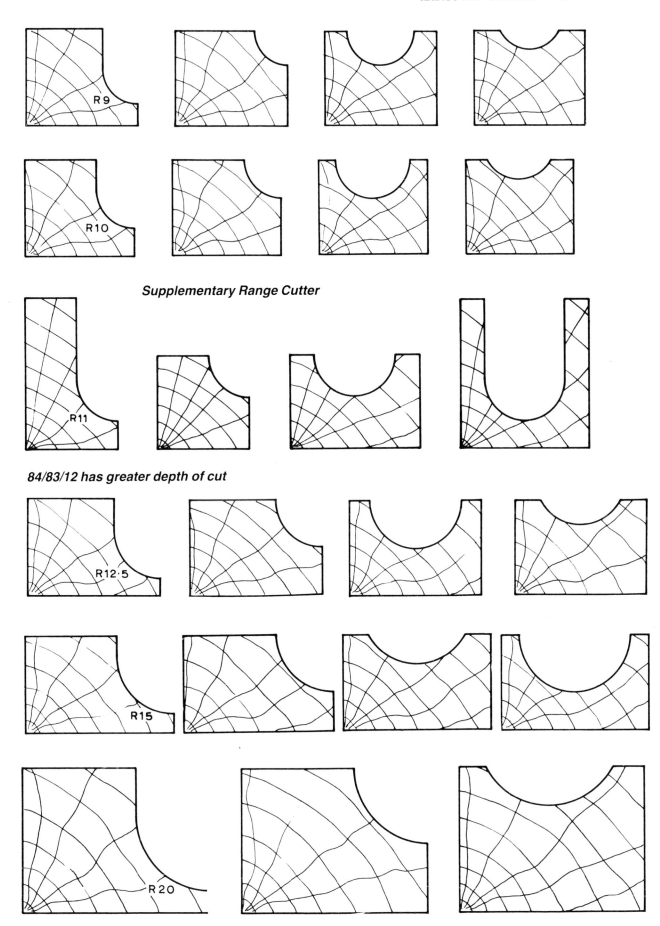

Supplementary Range Cutter

84/83/12 has greater depth of cut

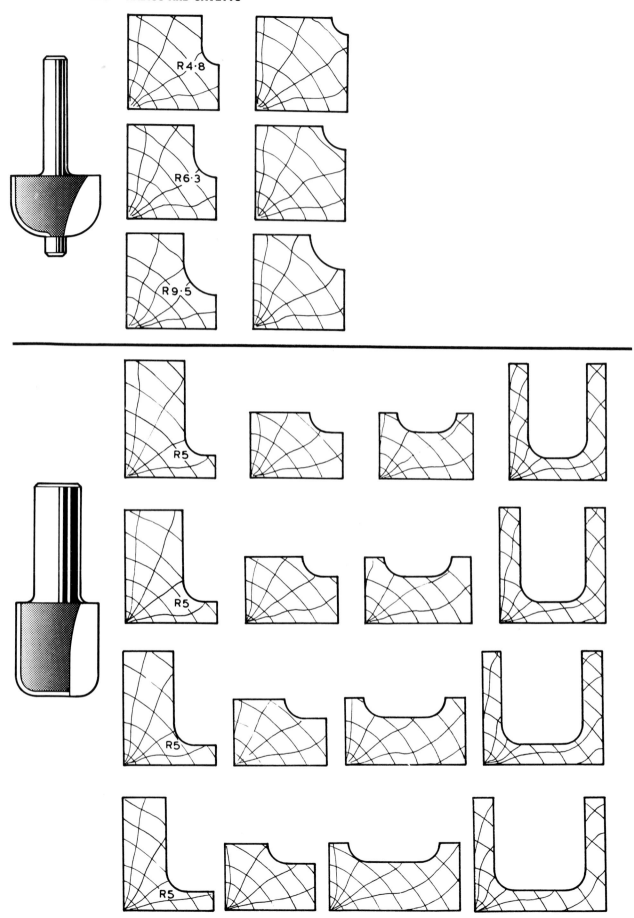

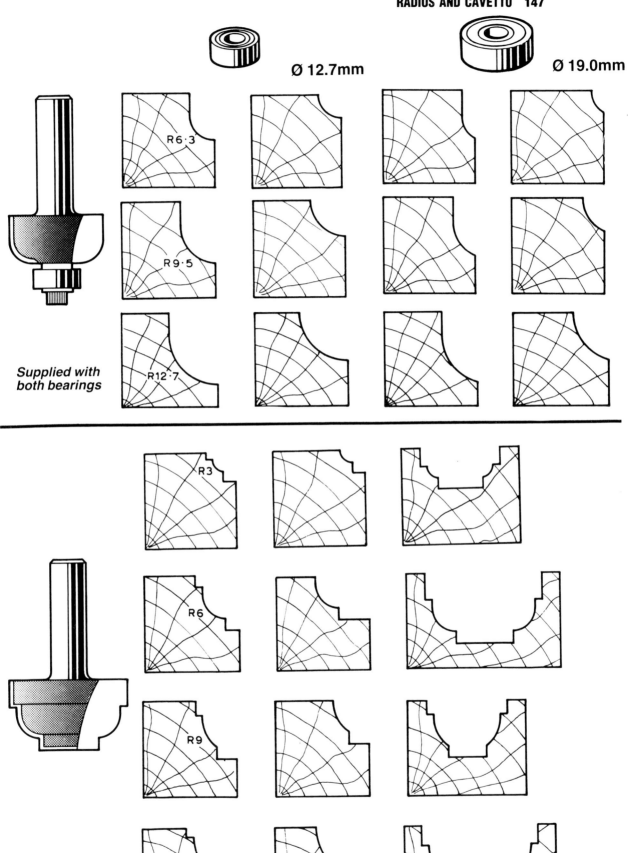

Ø 12.7mm

Ø 19.0mm

R6·3

R9·5

R12·7

Supplied with both bearings

R3

R6

R9

R13

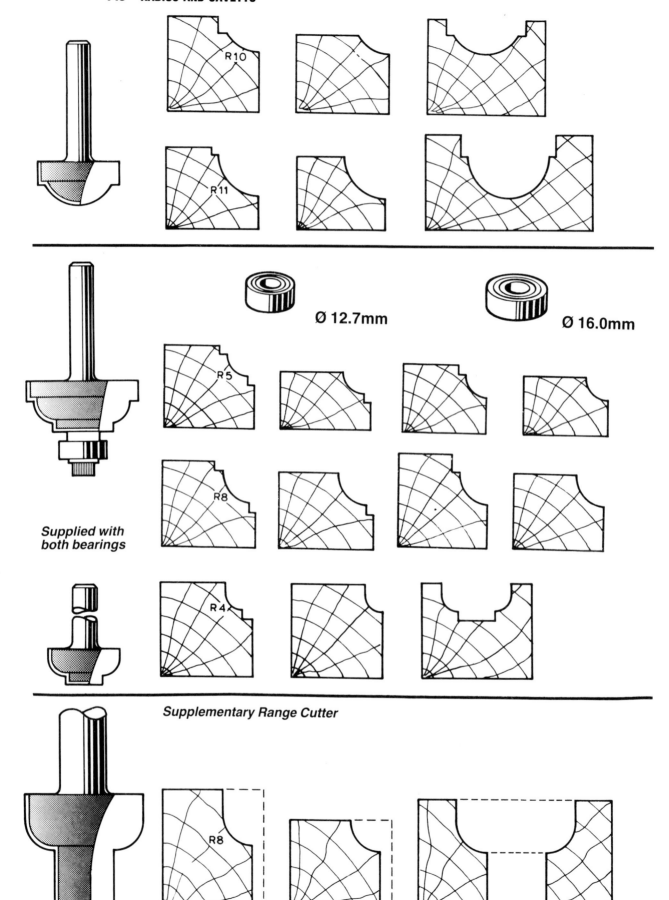

Ø 12.7mm

Ø 16.0mm

Supplied with both bearings

Supplementary Range Cutter

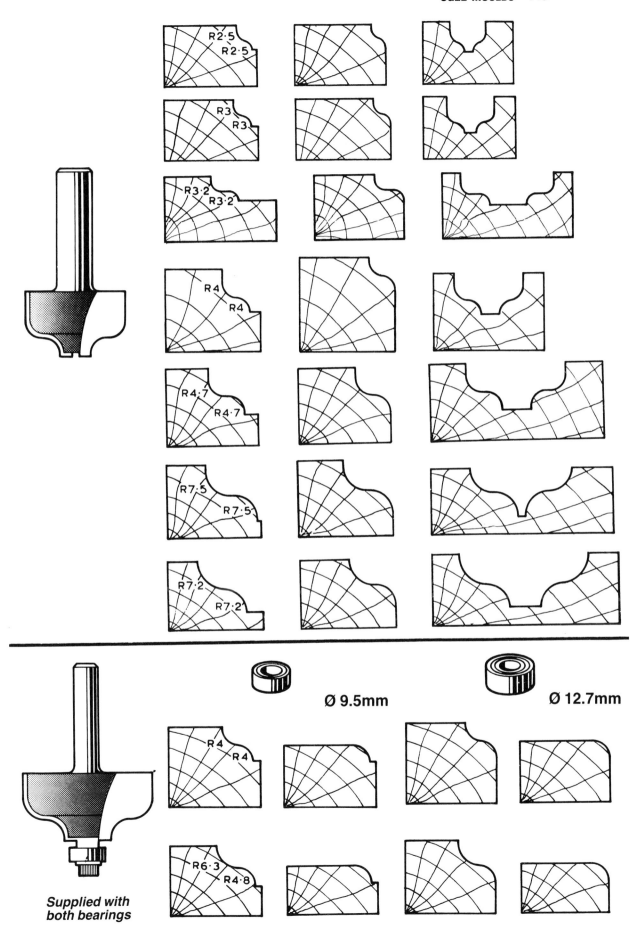

Ø 9.5mm

Ø 12.7mm

Supplied with both bearings

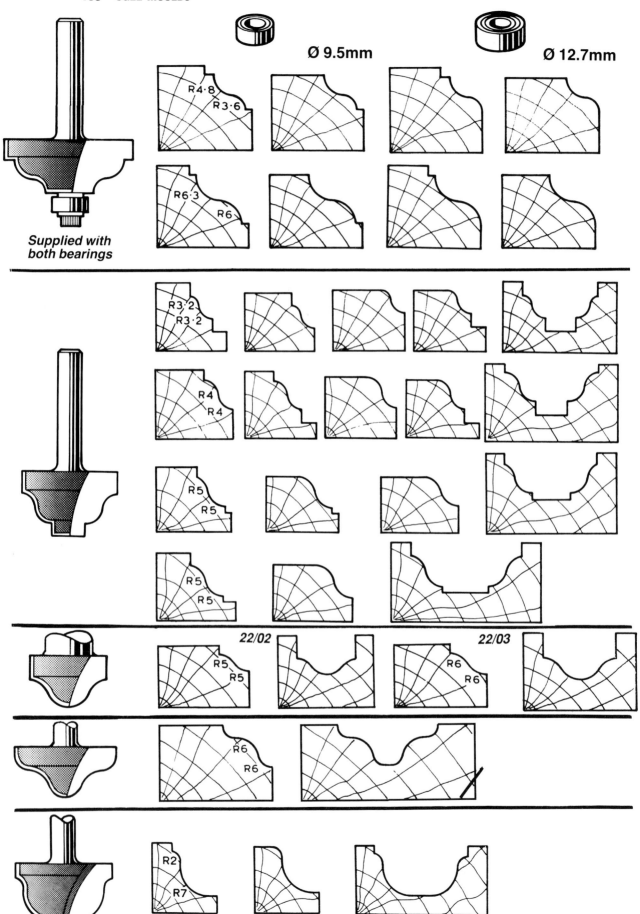

Ø 9.5mm

Ø 12.7mm

Supplied with both bearings

R4·8
R3·6

R6·3
R6

R3·2
R3·2

R4
R4

R5
R5

R5
R5

R5
R5

22/02

22/03

R5
R5

R6
R6

R6
R6

R2
R7

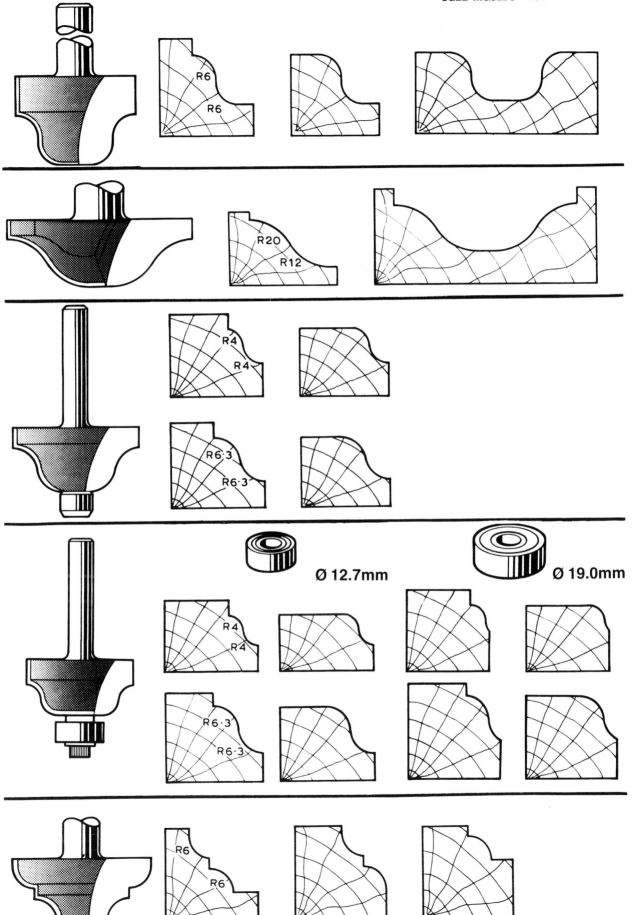

Ø 12.7mm

Ø 19.0mm

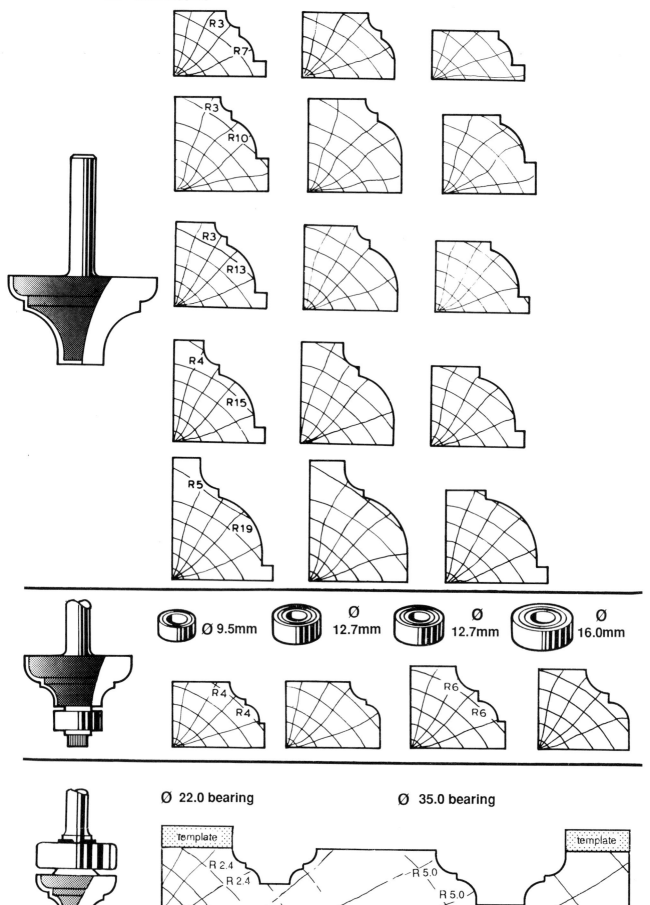

R 3
R 7

R 3
R 10

R 3
R 13

R 4
R 15

R 5
R 19

Ø 9.5mm   Ø 12.7mm   Ø 12.7mm   Ø 16.0mm

R 4
R 4

R 6
R 6

Ø 22.0 bearing   Ø 35.0 bearing

template   template

R 2.4
R 2.4

R 5.0
R 5.0

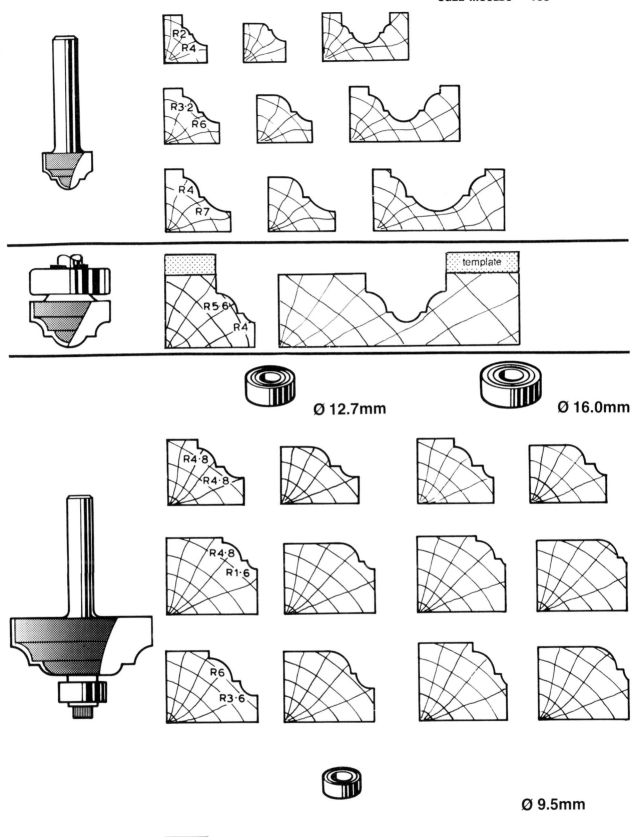

Ø 12.7mm

Ø 16.0mm

Ø 9.5mm

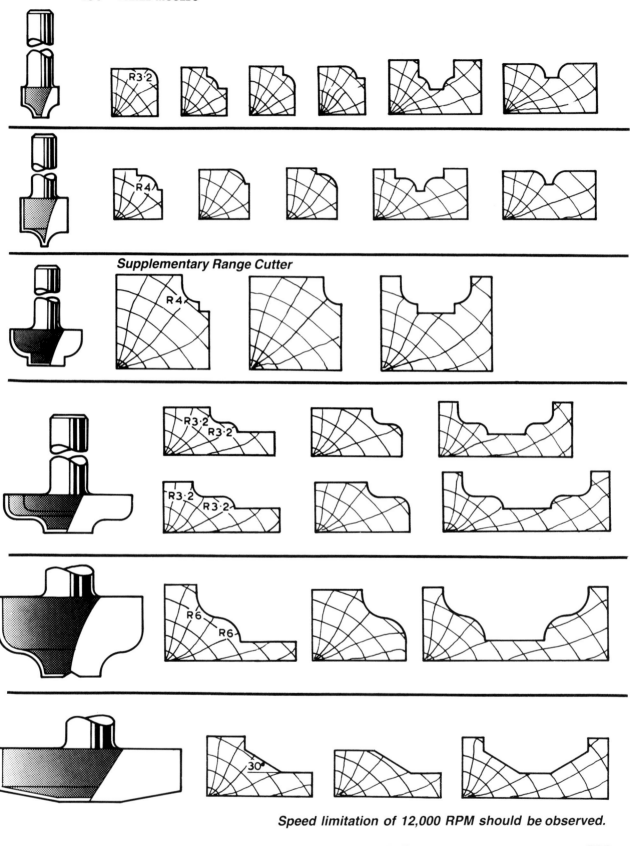

Supplementary Range Cutter

Speed limitation of 12,000 RPM should be observed.

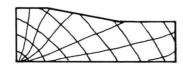

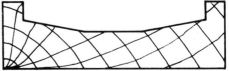

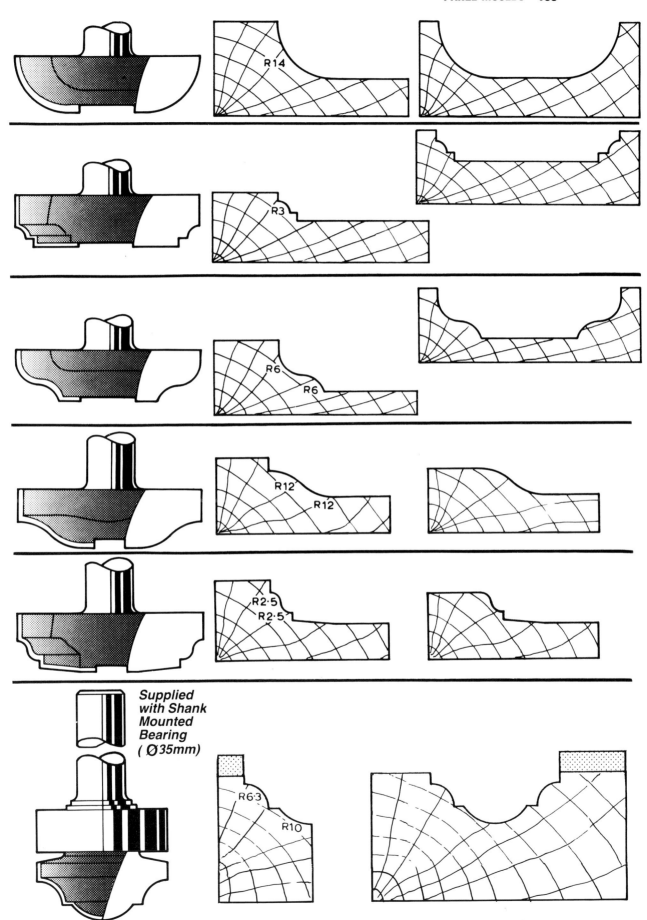

Supplied
with Shank
Mounted
Bearing
(Ø35mm)

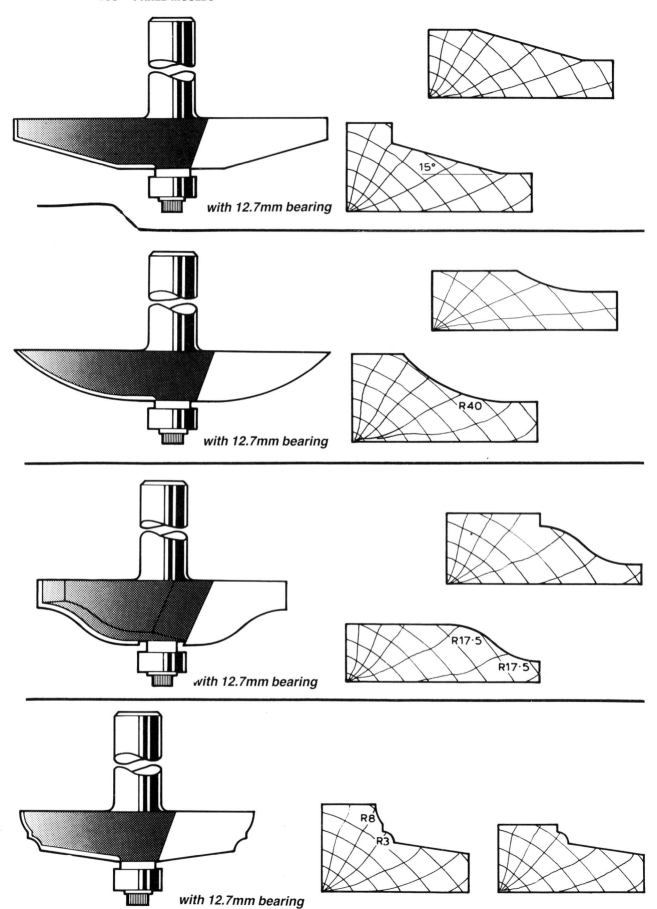

with 12.7mm bearing

15°

with 12.7mm bearing

R40

with 12.7mm bearing

R17·5
R17·5

with 12.7mm bearing

R8
R3

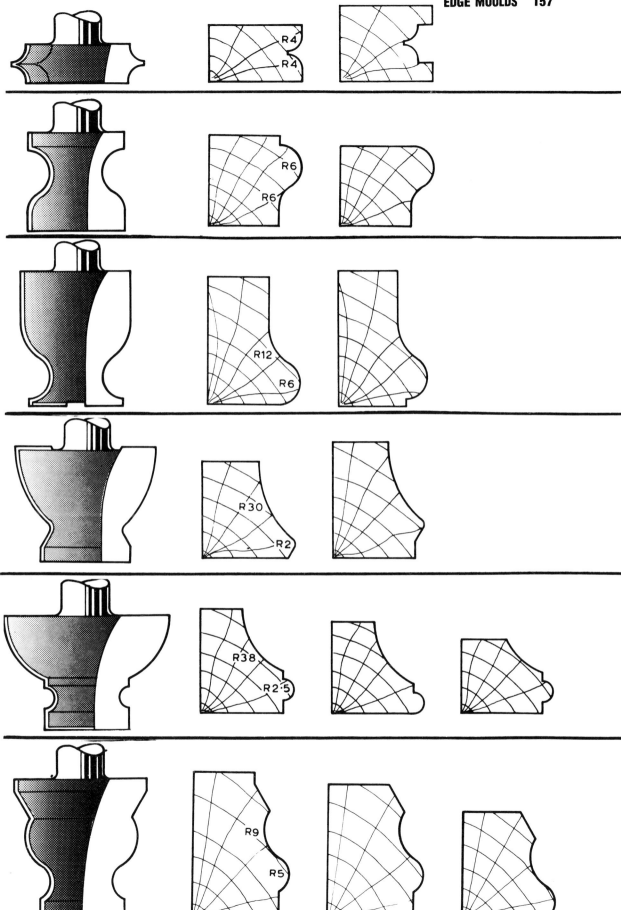

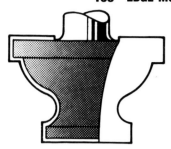 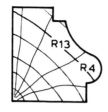 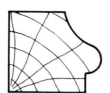 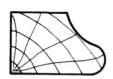

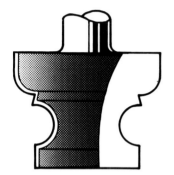 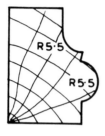  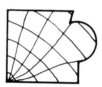

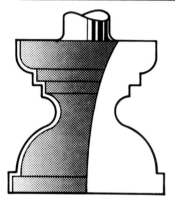 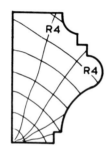 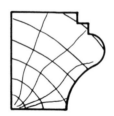 

 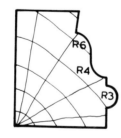 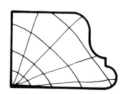

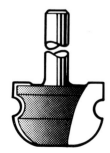 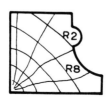 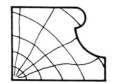

OVOLO JOINT SET

SASH BAR OVOLO SET

CLASSIC PANEL JOINT SET

TONGUED/BEAD JOINT SETS

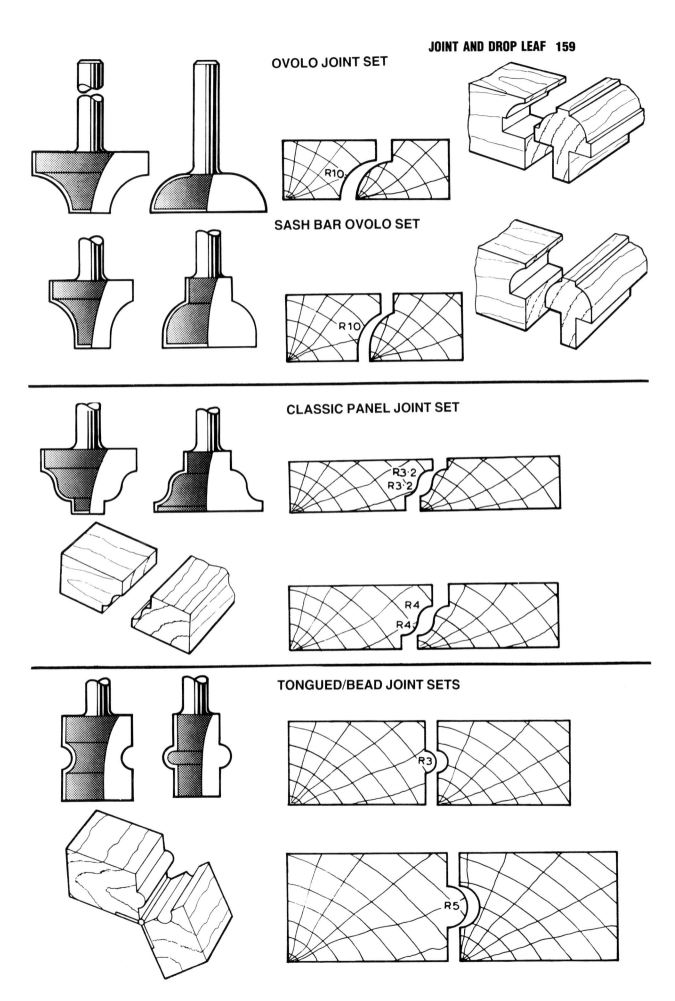

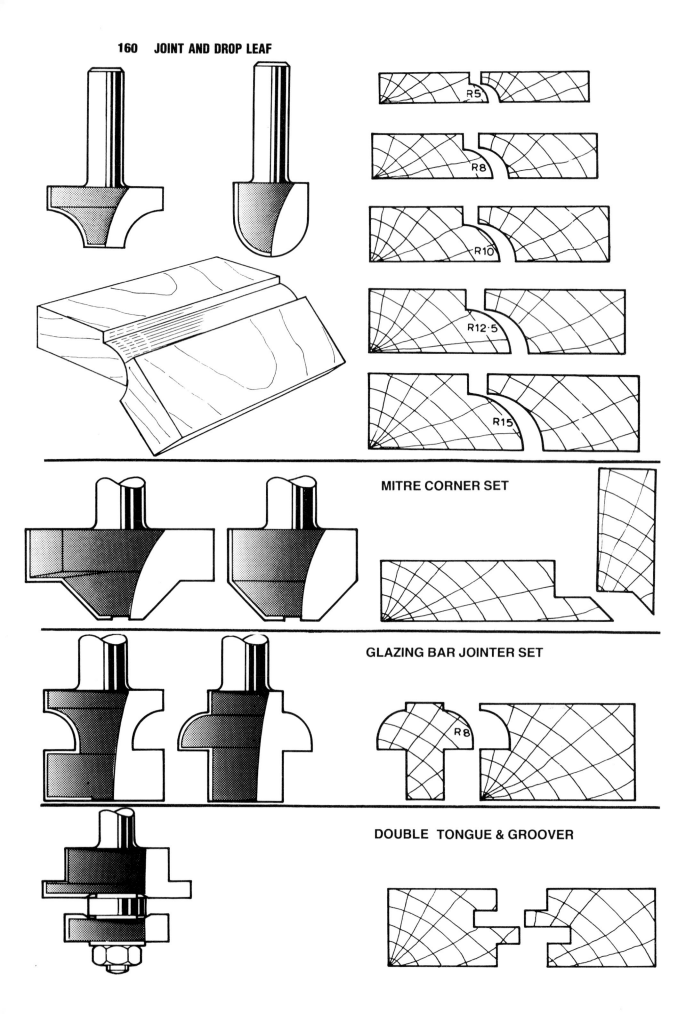

R5

R8

R10

R12·5

R15

MITRE CORNER SET

GLAZING BAR JOINTER SET

R8

DOUBLE TONGUE & GROOVER

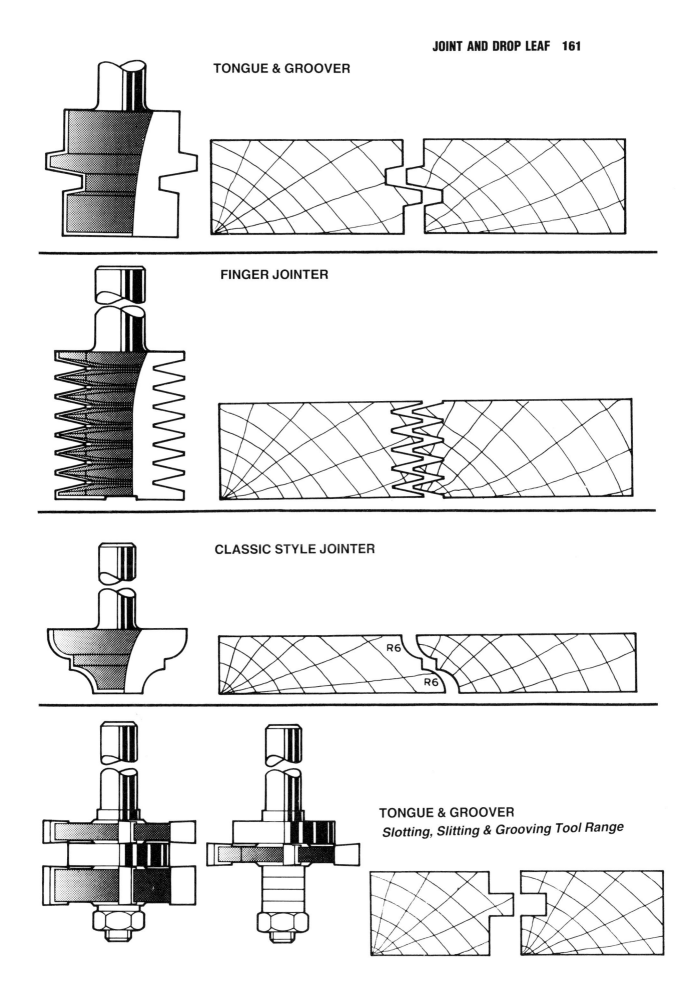

TONGUE & GROOVER

FINGER JOINTER

CLASSIC STYLE JOINTER

R6

R6

TONGUE & GROOVER
Slotting, Slitting & Grooving Tool Range

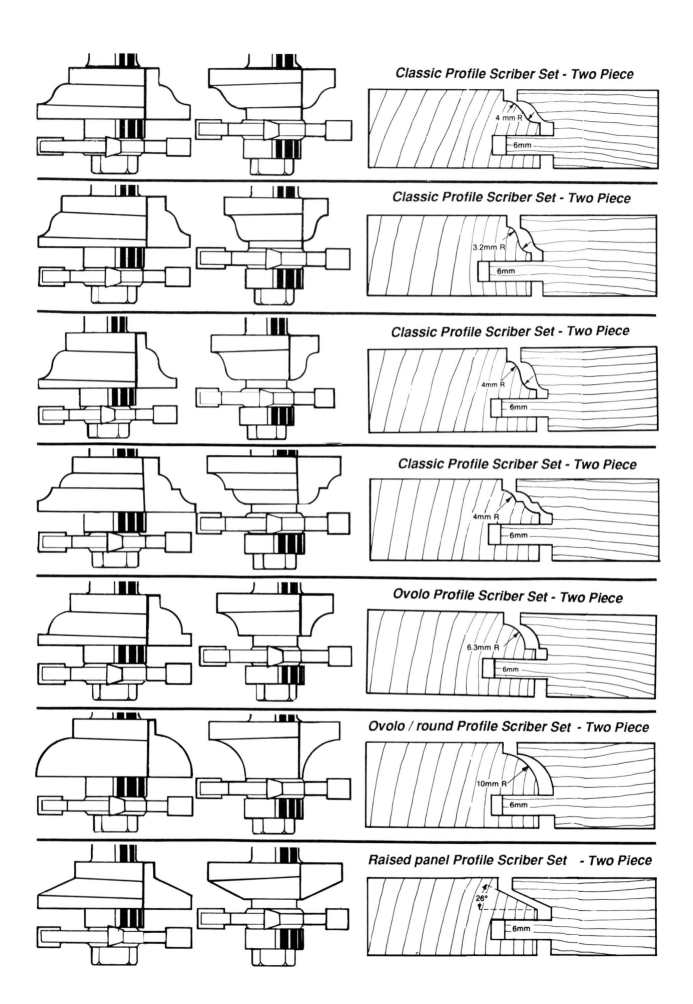

Classic Profile Scriber Set - Two Piece

4 mm R
6mm

Classic Profile Scriber Set - Two Piece

3.2mm R
6mm

Classic Profile Scriber Set - Two Piece

4mm R
6mm

Classic Profile Scriber Set - Two Piece

4mm R
6mm

Ovolo Profile Scriber Set - Two Piece

6.3mm R
6mm

Ovolo / round Profile Scriber Set - Two Piece

10mm R
6mm

Raised panel Profile Scriber Set - Two Piece

26°
6mm

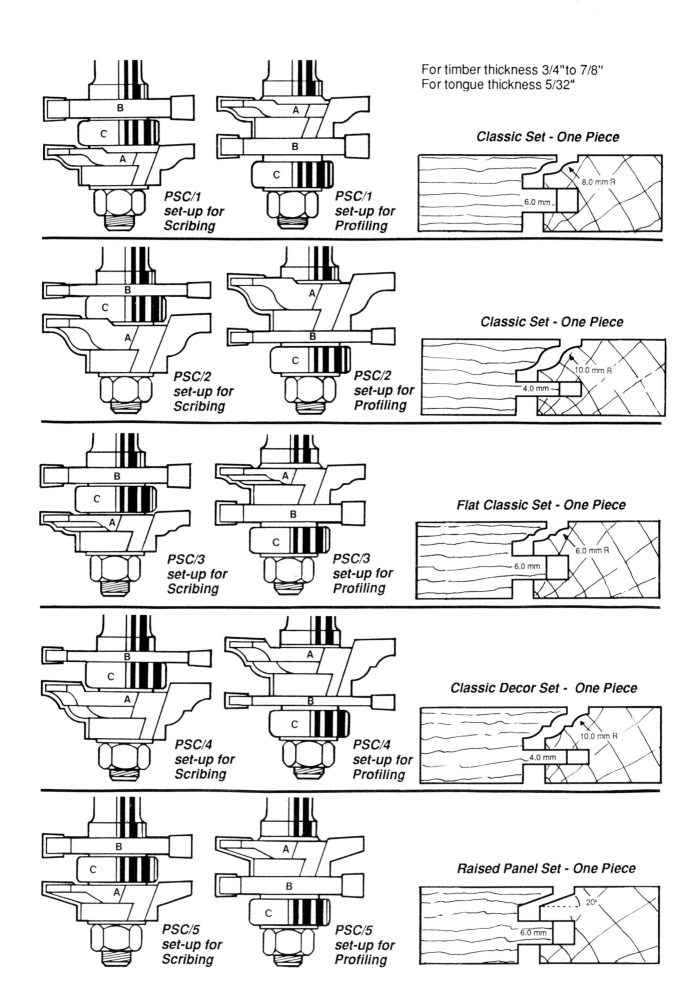

For timber thickness 3/4" to 7/8"
For tongue thickness 5/32"

PSC/1 set-up for Scribing

PSC/1 set-up for Profiling

Classic Set - One Piece

8.0 mm R
6.0 mm

PSC/2 set-up for Scribing

PSC/2 set-up for Profiling

Classic Set - One Piece

10.0 mm R
4.0 mm

PSC/3 set-up for Scribing

PSC/3 set-up for Profiling

Flat Classic Set - One Piece

6.0 mm R
6.0 mm

PSC/4 set-up for Scribing

PSC/4 set-up for Profiling

Classic Decor Set - One Piece

10.0 mm R
4.0 mm

PSC/5 set-up for Scribing

PSC/5 set-up for Profiling

Raised Panel Set - One Piece

20°
6.0 mm

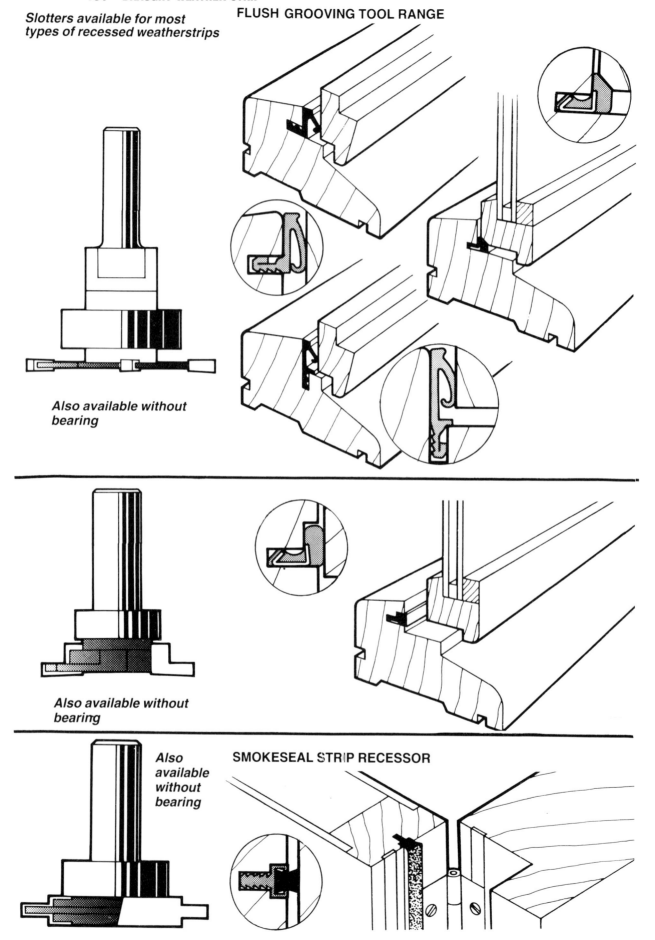

Slotters available for most types of recessed weatherstrips

FLUSH GROOVING TOOL RANGE

Also available without bearing

Also available without bearing

Also available without bearing

SMOKESEAL STRIP RECESSOR

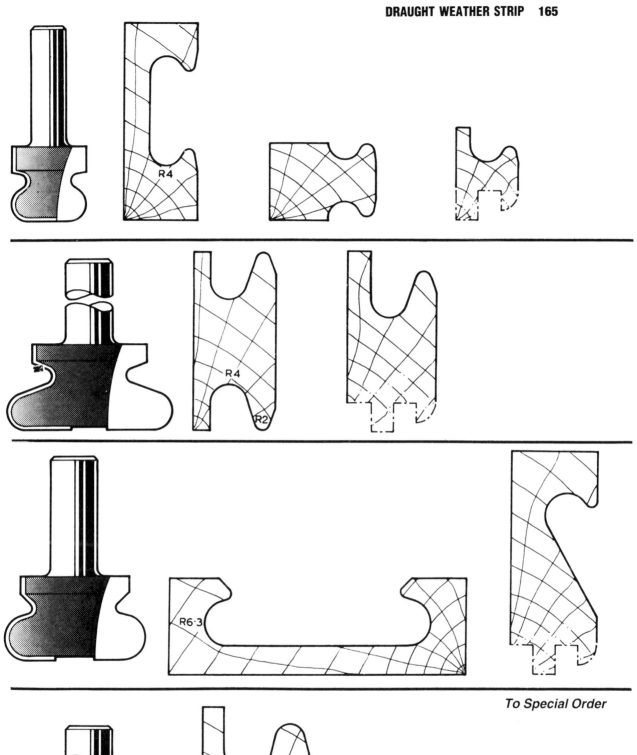

R4

R4

R2

R6·3

To Special Order

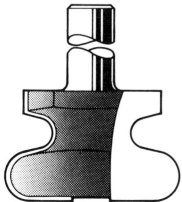

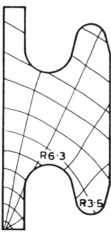

R6·3

R3·5

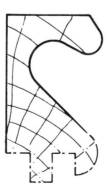

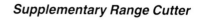

Supplementary Range Cutter

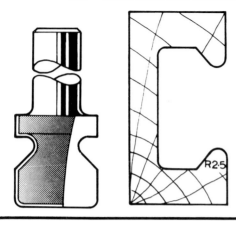

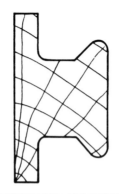

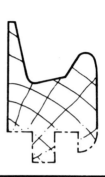

Supplementary Range Cutter

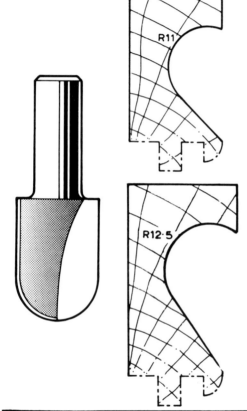

Supplementary Range Cutter

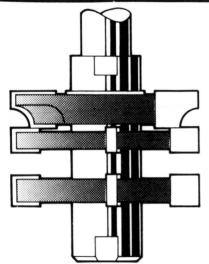

To Special Order

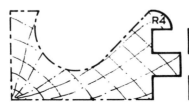

✻ *Plunge cut and profile facility*

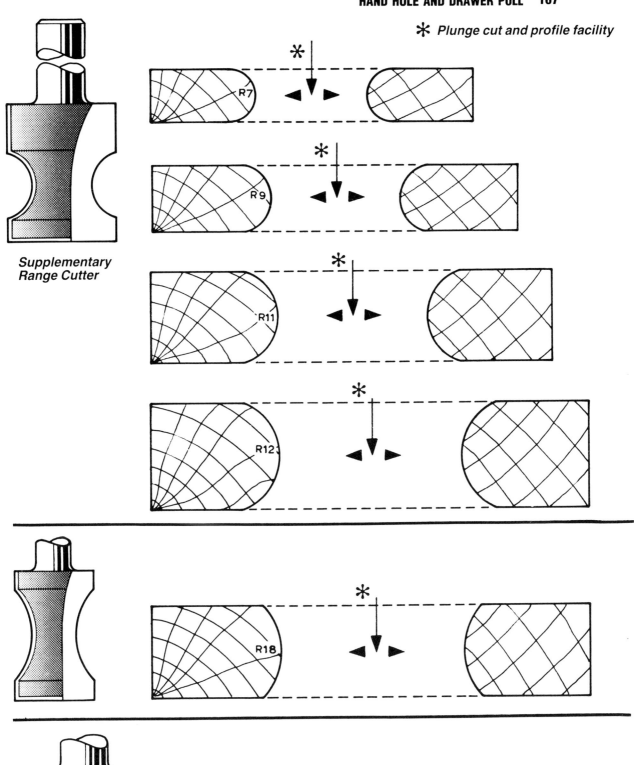

*Supplementary
Range Cutter*

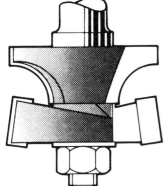

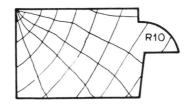

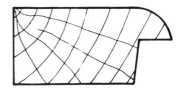

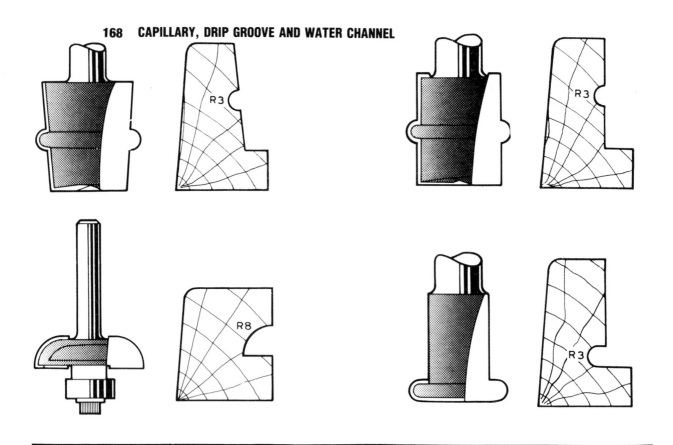

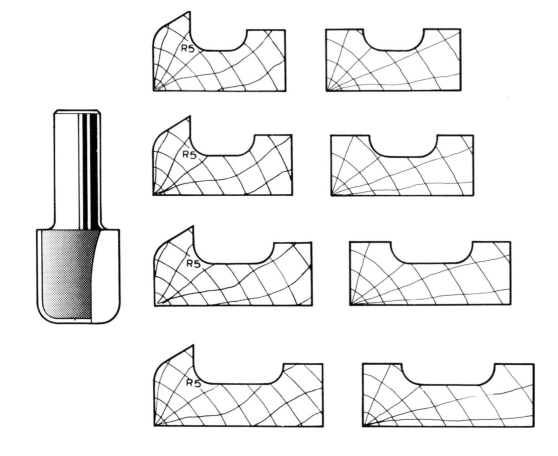

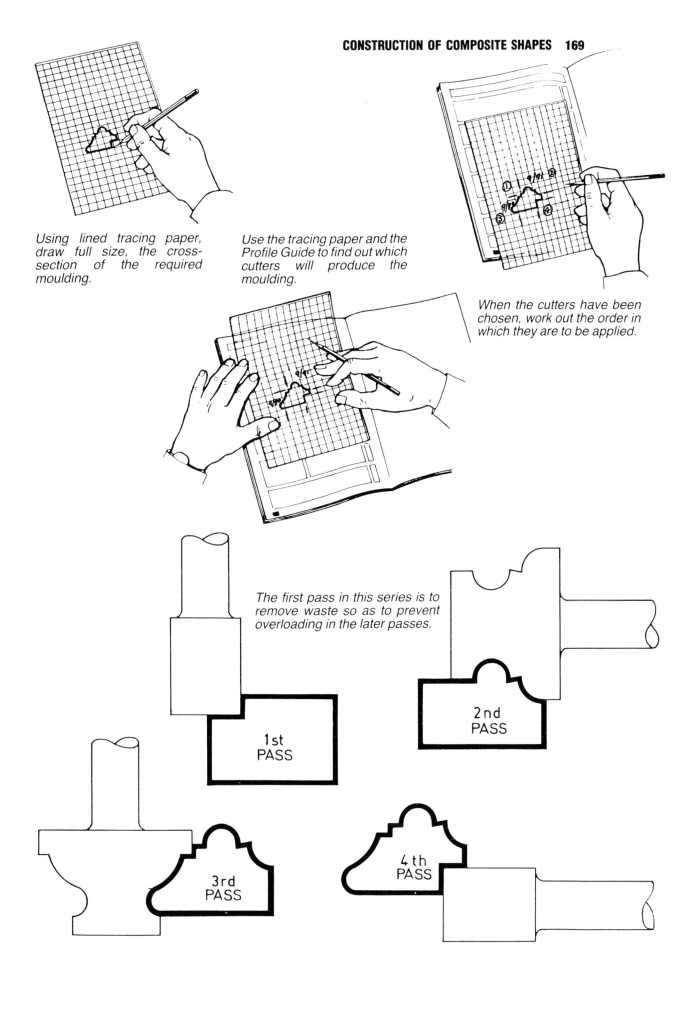

Using lined tracing paper, draw full size, the cross-section of the required moulding.

Use the tracing paper and the Profile Guide to find out which cutters will produce the moulding.

When the cutters have been chosen, work out the order in which they are to be applied.

The first pass in this series is to remove waste so as to prevent overloading in the later passes.

1st PASS

2nd PASS

3rd PASS

4th PASS

DOUBLE RAISED and FIELDED PANELS
DOORS etc

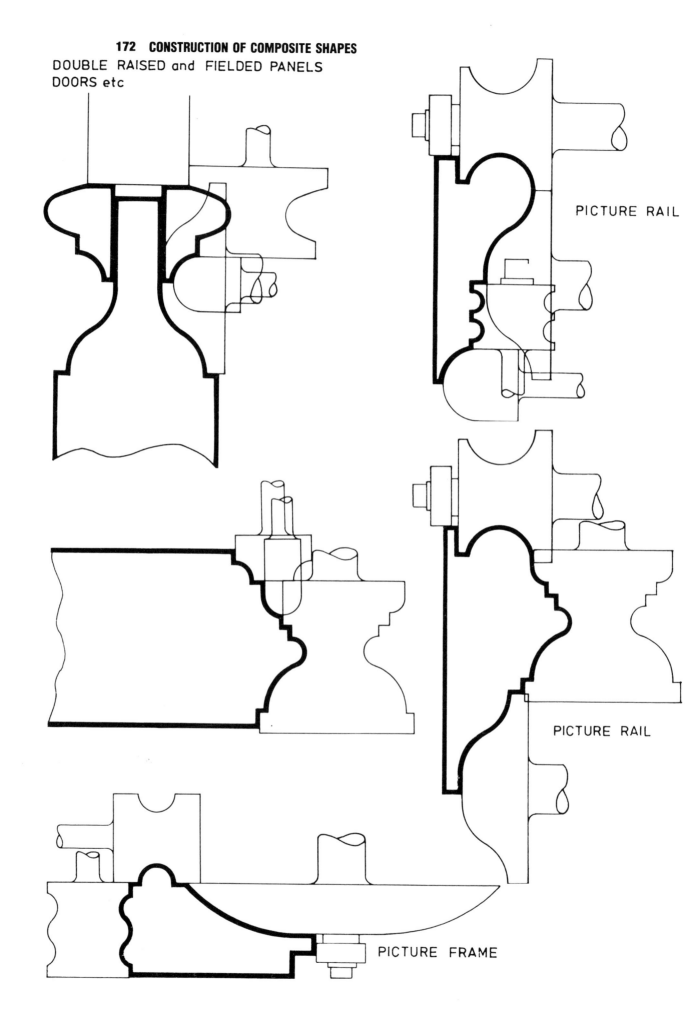

PICTURE RAIL

PICTURE RAIL

PICTURE FRAME

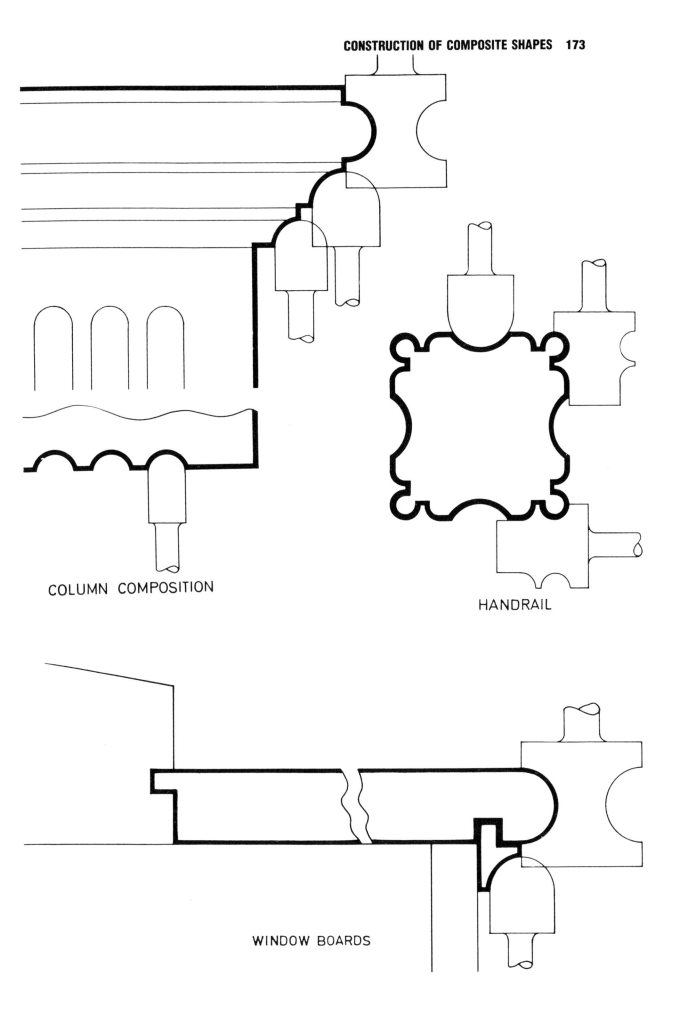

COLUMN COMPOSITION

HANDRAIL

WINDOW BOARDS